The Skeptical, Passionate Christian

*Tools for Living Faithfully
in an Uncertain World*

Michael F. Duffy

D0166883

Westminster John Knox Press
LOUISVILLE • LONDON

Scripture quotations, unless otherwise indicated, are from the New Revised Standard Version of the Bible, copyright © 1989 by the Division of Christian Education of the National Council of the Churches of Christ in the U.S.A., and used by permission.

Book design by Sharon Adams
Cover design by Eric Walljasper, Minneapolis, MN

First edition
Published by Westminster John Knox Press
Louisville, Kentucky

This book is printed on acid-free paper that meets the American National Standards Institute Z39.48 standard. ∞

PRINTED IN THE UNITED STATES OF AMERICA

06 07 08 09 10 11 12 13 14 15—10 9 8 7 6 5 4 3 2 1

Library of Congress Cataloging-in-Publication Data

Duffy, Michael Frederick.
    The skeptical, passionate Christian : tools for living faithfully in an uncertain world / Michael F. Duffy.— 1st ed.
        p. cm.
    Includes bibliographical references (p.   ).
    Contents: A skeptical, passionate faith — Defining faith and theology — Partners in Christian conversations — Exploring theological issues : basic steps — Vocation, part 1 : Developing a hypothesis — Vocation, part 2 : Conversations — God, love, and vocation.
    ISBN-13: 978-0-664-23008-1 (alk. paper)
    ISBN-10: 0-664-23008-3
    1. Theology—Methodology. 2. Vocation—Christianity. I. Title.

BR118.D84 2006
230—dc22

2005058462

The Skeptical, Passionate Christian

For my father, Donald Edward Duffy

For my mother, Laura Tiemann Duffy, may she rest in peace

For my sister, Margaret "Peggy" Duffy

Contents

Preface

I have a dilemma. On the one hand, I do not believe that we can be sure about what God is doing. On the other hand, I consider myself to be a committed Christian. How can I hold these two things—the skepticism and the passion—together and live as God wants me to live? The answer, of course, is: by faith. But faith in what? Theology is the process of answering the question, "Faith in what?" And vocation is one idea that Christians assess in the process of coming to understand how to live. These things are what this book is about.

I share some important parts of my life with you in these pages—not because you need to know about my life, but because I want to encourage you to think about theology and vocation at a very personal level. To that end, I try to show you how to think theologically and how to develop a personal theological point of view on issues that are important to all Christians. Most particularly, I explore the idea of vocation and show you how to discover what God is calling you to do.

I want to thank Kimberlee Maphis Early for supporting and encouraging this project. A couple of years ago, in her role as the coordinator of the Lilly Endowment's Programs for the Theological Exploration of Vocation, Kim called together several of us who were involved with the PTEV initiative for a discussion of the literature that might be commissioned in support of it. Among other things, it seemed important to have something written at an introductory theological level. I had started working on such a project at that point, and Kim urged me to continue it. She has been a blessing to me, in words and actions, at every step of the way.

My thanks, also, to Craig Dykstra and Christopher Coble at Lilly Endowment, Inc. Their leadership and Endowment support, along with the subsequent work of so many at colleges, universities, and seminaries around the country, has lifted the theological idea of vocation into the awareness of tens of thousands of students, teachers, adminstrators, writers, artists, and others. It can only be a good thing that so many of us are seeing God and our lives with new eyes.

I want to thank the members of the Department of Theological Studies at Hanover College, of which I am a part, for being both excellent intellectual colleagues and delightful friends. I am a far better teacher, thinker, writer, and Christian because of them. It is a joy to come to work each day and be surrounded by this group of people.

In addition to the Department—Philip Barlow, Michelle Bartel, J. David Cassel, Charles Quaintance, and G. David Yeager—many others have read and commented upon various parts of this work. My deep appreciation to all of these for helping me to see more clearly: Dulcinea Boesenberg, Steven Boone, Douglas Brash, David Buchman, Bonnie Chaplin, Kimberlee Maphis Early, Elise Erikson, Jay Hammon, Jane Jakoubek, Amy Jay, Katherine Johnson, Margaret Krantz, Annie Osterloh, Barry Penn-Hollar, Vickie Perkins, Carol Schoenberger Potochney, Michelle Gammon Purvis, Allison Rainey, Keet Redden, Rachel Ellison Schroeder, Amy Schultz, Lywin Kathryn Smith-Anderson, Gavin Stephens, Kay Stokes, Betty Uyesugi, Karla Van Zee, Becky Voyles, and Julie Witherup. Additional thanks go to the many students in many classes, both at James Madison University in Harrisonburg, Virginia, and at Hanover College in Hanover, Indiana, who have seen bits and pieces of these chapters over the last two decades. My deepest apologies to anyone I have forgotten.

My friends at the Attic Coffee Mill Café, in Madison, Indiana, have treated me like family in recent years, and that has been both fun and touching. I have spent a considerable number of hours at their counters and tables writing this book, staring out at the streets of Madison and trying to figure out what I wanted to say. Thanks to them for the coffee, salads, pie, and friendship.

In a book that draws heavily on aspects of my personal life, it is appropriate to name some of those who have been my mentors. I would single out Don Giroux, a high school social studies teacher who, by example and nurturing, set the tone of my intellectual and spiritual life; Father Richard E. Crews, who showed me what I wanted to be when I grew up; James F. Childress, whose guidance made all the difference many times and in innumerable ways; and Joseph F. Fletcher, whose work, heart, and presence I will always remember and always admire.

I thank my parents and sister, to whom this book is dedicated, for being my original community of discernment. I thank my friend Kelly, from whom I have learned much about living faithfully. I thank Bonnie, who has been amazingly patient with my writing process. And I thank Nicole Smith Murphy. Nicki is my editor at Westminster John Knox Press. Nicki was a theological studies major at Hanover not many years ago. She has become a good friend and, now, my insightful and fun editor. Much of the clarity of this book is due to her excellent guidance. Thank you for your enthusiasm, Nicole.

1

A Skeptical, Passionate Faith

The death of my mother a decade ago gave me a new and deeper awareness of the struggle that lies at the core of faith. On the one hand, my own Christian faith is central to my life and to my work. I grew up in the church, spent a decade as a church pastor, served for three years as the chaplain at a church-related college, and now teach Christian theology and ethics there. I am thankful that God loves me, and I do my best to follow the commands of Jesus to love God and my neighbors. I pray daily, and I regularly practice one or more of the disciplines that are typically considered to be central to Christian life, including worship, meditation, intercession, confession, Bible study, and charitable giving. At the same time, however, I am convinced that we cannot be certain about God's actions and purposes. We cannot be certain that the characteristics we attribute to God are indeed God's characteristics. We cannot know for sure that anything we say about God is true of God. We cannot know with certainty that what we think God wants us to do, individually or in our various communities, is actually what God wants us to do. How is it possible to think and live as Christians, despite awareness that much of what we believe and do may be out of touch with reality? That is what this book is about.

I hope you will resist the urge to answer this question with the quick assertion that all I am doing is pointing out what we already know about faith, namely, that it is belief without certainty. As one of my colleagues likes to say, that would be a "partial credit" answer. Even if that were a good definition of faith, which it is not, we would still be left with the question of how we can make sense out of having to live in this way. Even more importantly, it seems clear that the current world in which we live finds this dilemma to be so impossible that one option is often chosen and asserted with no accountability and no critical assessment. Too many of us simply want to assert aggressively our own theological and religious points of view, while others of us argue that the acknowledgment of uncertainty leads to the death of theology and religion. In contrast, through the course of this book we will see that passionate faith and critical analysis are not only compatible but together can help us to live together more abundantly.

At several points during my introductory courses in theology, I remind students that the questions we consider there—who or what God is, what life means, how we should treat one another, what each of us is to do with his or her unique life—are among the most important questions that can be asked. Their focus is on our fundamental orientation to life, the basic stance we take when we face the world. How each one of us responds to these questions will shape significant parts of the life we have before us. If, for example, it is true that we live not only in relationship to one another, but to a God who loves us and invites us to respond to that love, our daily life takes on a different meaning from the meaning it would have were there no such God. While we might begin to explore and answer these questions in several ways, thereby developing a personal theological vision, I like to begin by having students think autobiographically.

Telling the story of one's life and one's faith does not provide direct insight into the nature of God. Saying that I felt peace in my heart when I asked God for peace does not lead inevitably to the conclusion that God gave me peace. Healing from a horrible illness when I was not expected to live does not mean that God healed me. The facts that I believe something to be true or that someone has told me that something is true are not guarantees that those things are in fact true. However, beginning to explore theological questions by looking at our lives sets the stage for critically developing our own theological view and resolving the struggle we face between faith and uncertainty. When we correlate aspects of our personal histories with aspects of our theological points of view, we have a starting point for the journey ahead. I encourage you, as you move through these chapters, to ponder the relationship between your life story and your religious views. Since I know my own life best, I illustrate the theological process with references to my own story.

I grew up in rural Connecticut and spent many summers and school vacations working on a dairy farm down the road from us. Between 1960 and 1962, my father built the house in which I spent most of my childhood on land given to him by his parents, my grandparents. He was and is a land surveyor and carries values characteristic of someone from a lower-middle-class rural environment who lived through the Depression and fought in the Second World War. He is a hard-working, moral, and faithful Christian man. My mother only occasionally worked outside the home. She was the person primarily responsible for child care, and I remember her spending lots of active time with my younger sister and me in our earliest years. We biked and swam and enjoyed life. Somewhere around the time I entered first grade or a little after, Mom was stricken with an illness that I experienced as physically and emotionally distancing her, in some ways, for several decades.

My childhood was about school and church. Encouraged by both parents, I loved school, loved reading and learning, did well, and indeed, have never left. Through college, three graduate programs, and a career in academia, school has always been a place of nurturing for me. Church was St. Andrew's Episcopal down the street, the church in which Dad was raised and his mother played the organ. I was an acolyte and president of the small youth fellowship, sang (though not well) in the junior choir, and found in the church a second home, a place of safety, affirmation, and faith. I believed in the God of the *Book of Common Prayer* and the Bible, was the only member of a senior high Bible study class, and, though I certainly asked lots of questions, was at least temporarily satisfied with the answers of the church.

When I was about twelve, I received what I would later come to view as a call to the ministry. One Sunday morning, I was the acolyte of the day and began to lead the choir up the center aisle during the processional hymn. Suddenly, I was up above the altar, at the top of the church, looking down and watching myself walk up the aisle. I was processing and could see myself, but I was somehow more above the altar than walking up the aisle. Accompanying this out-of-body experience was a clear sense of being at home. The church, I then knew, was the place I would spend my life in service to God and God's people. I resolved to attend seminary and enter the ministry.

By the time I headed off to Hartwick College, a small liberal arts college in Oneonta, New York, I was still focused on ministry, but I majored in philosophy, a discipline with which I had become enamored during my junior year in high school. Throughout the next four years, two at Hartwick and two at the University of Massachusetts at Amherst, I wandered among interests in philosophy, linguistics, and psychology, generally coming back to philosophy. I enjoyed the subject so much that I decided that I would go to graduate school for a Ph.D. in it and teach it for a living instead of entering the ministry. Halfway through my master's degree, I decided that the life of the professional philosopher was not for me, so I left the University of North Carolina at Chapel Hill after two years and went to seminary at Harvard Divinity School.

My late high school and college years were characterized by faith exploration. I briefly engaged a wide variety of New Age resources. I pondered God, but hardly ever went to church unless I was home in Connecticut or visiting a friend. I met a wonderful Mormon girl and explored the Mormon version of Christianity. In the year between college and graduate school, I worked in a factory and saved money for a trip to Scotland and England, spending the first of my five weeks there living and working in the Findhorn community in northern Scotland. During parts of this time, the intention to enter the ministry remained; during other parts, I wanted to do philosophy or linguistics or psychology; during other parts, I had no idea what I wanted to do. I had fun learning whatever I was studying, playing guitar, hanging out with friends, spending lots of time with the girlfriend of the moment, and the like.

I remember asking God during the end of my first year and beginning of my second at Chapel Hill whether I should attend seminary. It seemed to me that God should make the answer clear if God really wanted me to go into the ministry. I kept praying, kept asking for a sign, kept wanting for God to do something obvious and spectacular to show me I should go. And then one day, sitting at my desk working on something else, it occurred to me that I already had the sign. The depth of the desire that lay behind my fervent prayer was itself my sign. In the facts that I wanted deeply to go, that so much of my life had focused on this plan, that friends and family had encouraged this direction, that I was ready to go, that God was clearing the path, I already had my sign. I applied, was accepted, and moved to Cambridge.

Divinity school was wonderful in every way. It was three uninterrupted years of focus on God, on the things that had always mattered most to me. It was a merging of my heart and my head into the possibilities of ministry and the challenge of making sense of the world. While in Chapel Hill, I had moved from the Episcopal Church to the United Church of Christ, and it was the latter denomination with which I remained associated. But I soon found myself with another tug of the heart and, following Harvard Divinity, I moved to Charlottesville to do a Ph.D. in theological ethics at the University of Virginia.

Since memory becomes clearer, at least in quantity, the closer I come to the present day, I could now write for many pages about the time since I moved to Charlottesville in 1984. It has been twenty years, but the time has flown by. There have been many hard times and many good times. The good times include some wonderful relationships all along the way, a thoroughly enjoyable Ph.D. experience with tremendous faculty and colleagues who remain friends, living in excellent cities and towns, steady and supportive relationships with my parents and sister. The bad times include the ending of a serious relationship, the death of my mother, a divorce, and occasional bouts with anxiety and depression that used to drive me to the brink of giving up. I try here to capture four moments in time that may provide meaningful reference points for later parts of this discussion—two moments of calling, two moments of losing.

A year into my doctoral course work, I received a phone call from the Rev. Dr. Bernie Zerkel, Associate Conference Minister for the Shenandoah Association of the U.C.C. He wondered if I would like to do some supply preaching. Later, having preached weekly at Bethlehem U.C.C. for two years, I picked up my mail at the post office one day and walked along Charlottesville's Downtown Mall reading a letter from Bernie in which he asked if I would consider becoming the full-time pastor of the church. Tears streamed from my eyes as it seemed to me that God was calling through Bernie's letter, and it would be another eight years before I left that congregation.

In 1995, I moved to Hanover College in Hanover, Indiana, to be its chaplain. Upon the retirement of the senior member of the Department of Theological Studies three years later, the question arose of whether I would become the department's full-time theological ethicist. Conversations with colleagues, friends, my wife, the academic dean, and the president of the college; examination of my own motives and strengths and weaknesses; reflection upon my ministry to that point; a search inward for what I loved and outward for how others responded to me in the classroom—all of these things combined gave me the sense, which has continued ever since, that teaching here in this place is indeed what I am called to do.

In the midst of this journey, I faced two huge losses. A matter of days before I was to interview at Hanover, my mother died. So many of the positive contributions I make to the world are a direct response to her example and teaching, and so many of my struggles in life are related to my sense of her emotional withdrawal when I was a child. Her death was particularly difficult because of the renewed and deepened relationship we had in her last few years of life. Four years later, my wife and I divorced. This loss was almost unbearable and fed into several bouts of anxiety and depression. I have often thought that she was right to leave in the sense that it enabled her to live the life she needed to live, but her friendship and companionship were an enormous loss. Together, these experiences made me extremely aware of my fear of abandonment and the anxiety and disorientation I can feel at any hint of rejection or loss.

If you have been reviewing your own life along with reading mine, I invite you to think about how the moments you remembered are relevant to your theological understandings. For me, the precise connections are difficult to assess, as I suggested earlier, but there are important questions I must ask. Am I enabled to see the presence of God because of my longing for the presence of the other, or, in contrast, is it my longing that leads me to cling to a model of God as present? If I go through anxiety and depression and feel God as not present, does this say something about me or about God or both? How would I decide between the two? How does my rural upbringing shape my understanding of God? Does it enable me to see God's role in nature more fully, or does it cause me to want to believe in a God who is involved in nature? When tears stream down my cheek upon reading a letter, is this really the result of God calling, or am I simply happy to be loved or wanted? If my mother dies at a young age (sixty-one) and my divorce happens while I have been praying that neither will occur, does this suggest there is no God who answers prayer, that God answers but not always in ways we like, that I was praying the wrong prayers, or that the whole notion of a God who answers prayers and intervenes in the world is simply the creation of my heart and the heart of others before me who have needed God in their own ways? As I suggested earlier, I do not believe we can know with certainty the answers to these questions, but I do believe that the universe poses similar questions to each one of us and that life is better lived if we attempt to answer them and answer them well. In doing this, we define our basic stance toward life and can give ourselves over to that stance with a whole heart.

The themes that have been discussed in this chapter are developed more fully in the chapters ahead; they are the groundwork for everything that comes next. The next three chapters—on faith and theology, on the Christian's conversation partners, and on the steps of theological exploration—develop more fully what it means to think theologically. These chapters contain the tools that allow you to make thinking and living as a Christian part of your life's work. Chapter 5 begins the investigation of vocation and discerning what God is calling you to do by beginning to apply the steps from chapter 4. The final two chapters continue this exploration and, in the end, consider what it means to live moment by moment in faithfulness to God.

To end this beginning with a declaration of the faith that motivates this book, my deepest conviction is that the love that is the heart of the universe calls us to love one another. Even though I do not and cannot know that with certainty, I am committed to it as the best way to live life. I am, with Paul in Romans 8, convinced that nothing separates us from the love of God but, again, I say that without certainty. What I know for sure is that I have this life. That knowledge makes this life important, and my heart says there is nothing more important in life than rejecting all forms of dishonesty, exclusivity, deception, indifference, and malice, while expressing caring for one another and creating supportive, mutually loving relationships. That is the end toward which this book aims, but with the added hope that life lived this way does indeed reflect reality at its deepest. Even if there is no God, and no love at the heart of the universe, even if there were no Jesus of Nazareth, I still stake all I am on the conviction that the meaning of our lives is to love one another. To the extent that we do this, we live. To the extent we do not, we die.

Going Deeper

At this point, some of you might wish to skip ahead to the questions at the end of this chapter or even to chapter 2. You have now thought a bit about your own life, and you have been introduced to the ideas on which the following chapters are built. You may wish to jump right in to thinking about the nature of faith and theology. On the other hand, for those of you who would like to think more carefully and more deeply about a few of the issues involved in this project, the remainder of this chapter explores three of them: what it means to be a Christian, the nature of uncertainty, and the process of theological construction. Whichever direction you choose, you can always back up and head the other way if you find that it would be more helpful to you.

Being a Christian

What I have said to this point suggests that I believe it is important for every human being, not only Christians, to establish a personal theological stance. I do believe this, but the scholarly issues involved in defending such a claim are well beyond the scope of this work. With that in mind, I do not suggest that the claims I make here are universally applicable; in particular, I do not intend to suggest that the arguments I make and responses I offer are valid within all of the world's many faith traditions. Instead, I write here as a Christian primarily to other Christians and to anyone who may be exploring what it means to think carefully about life and God within a Christian context.

At the same time, I hope that people who are outside the Christian context find this work engaging. Later, I have occasion to discuss the importance of the study of other faith traditions not only for deepening one's own spiritual and religious life but also as part of the crucial project of seeking global human flourishing. Here, it seems appropriate simply to mention that discussions within particular faith traditions still make claims about the way the world is. These claims invite response from those who see the world differently, in the hope that discussion of different perspectives can lead us closer to making sense of the world and living together well.

In addition to the scholarly reasons for addressing this discussion primarily to an audience interested in thinking from within a Christian framework, there are personal reasons. Simply put, the Christian tradition provides me with the lenses and vehicles by which I make sense of my world. When I ponder questions of morality, I turn to the teachings of Jesus, to the meaning of the crucifixion, to the wisdom of the saints. When I stand in awe of the beauty of nature, I understand my experience in terms of God's creation. When I pray, worship, and face the mysteries of life, I do it in terms that come from Christianity. In some important sense, this choice is not mine. Speaking as a Christian, it is the Christian faith to which God has called me, through my lifelong immersion, to commit my life. Is it just that I do not know any other traditions well enough to choose them? Is it just that church felt like home to me in times when I did not feel home as home? Is it that I get something—security or affirmation, for example—from participation in the church? All these are true, but not true enough; I think the truth is deeper than these things. Indeed, I am committed to the view that God calls me to be a Christian; by the end of this book, I hope to have made clear what I mean by saying that.

One could legitimately feel at this point that focusing this project in a Christian context is not much of a focus, given the many differences that exist between Christians in the modern world. Given the wide doctrinal and moral gulfs that separate Christians, what can it mean to label a context of discussion as "Christian"? Here, it seems to me important to be as inclusive as possible. Broadly speaking, then, this book is addressed to those who somehow put Jesus of Nazareth at the center of their spiritual life and those who wish to understand what this means.

Uncertainty

I said at the beginning of this chapter that we cannot be certain about God's reality, nature, actions, characteristics, or purposes. In the jargon of the academy, this is an epistemological claim. Epistemology is simply the study of what we can and cannot know. Anyone who wishes to think about God (indeed, anyone who wishes to think about much of anything at all) would do well to begin with epistemological considerations. Epistemological issues are relevant to this book in at least three ways. The first is philosophical and concerns the possibility of human knowing. The second is theological and concerns the supposed nature of God. The third is more empirical and concerns my experience as a Christian theologian and person of faith.

Philosophically speaking, my view is that we should accept a form of what the academy today might call postmodern epistemology. To call anything "postmodern" is to encourage a great deal of unhelpful conversation, so let me quickly say what I mean and note that I mean it whether or not anyone wishes to use the term "postmodern" to describe it.

Postmodernism, as I mean it here, is a rejection of modern, Enlightenment approaches to knowing. As a type, the modern person believes he or she can know many things with great certainty, and that he or she can assess and evaluate things from an objective standpoint, a standpoint sufficiently distant from what is being evaluated so that the process of evaluation, of coming to know, is not unduly influenced. Postmodernism rejects this modern, Enlightenment confidence in both the certainty and the objectivity of knowledge. For the postmodernist, we do not know what we know with certainty; we only know what we know relative to the tradition within which our knowledge is articulated. There is no firm place to stand outside of our traditions that would provide us with the possibility of purely objective discernment. That is, for the postmodernist, there is no place I can stand, as a human being who is a product of my own upbringing and other cultural influences, that will enable me to see Reality with clarity, and any "certainty" I achieve is a certainty only within and with respect to the traditions and communities of which I am a part. Thus, Christian affirmations, for example, are not objective certainties; there is no guarantee of their truth outside of the framework of the Christian tradition within which they arose and within which they are articulated and lived.

It is important not to overstate the implications of these claims; specifically, there are three conclusions we should be careful not to draw. The first is that there is no Reality, no Truth with a capital "T." To say that we cannot know with certainty the nature of this Reality is not to say that it does not exist. We are talking here about human knowing, not the nature of being (epistemology, not ontology). Second, to say that we cannot know something with certainty is not to say that our claims about it are false; it is simply to say that we cannot know that they are true. For example, it may be true that God loves me and I may believe that God loves me, but I cannot know with certainty that God loves me. Such certainty is precluded by the influence of history, culture, traditions, and other shaping mechanisms on my life. Put another way, I might, given a certain set of assumptions and a certain context, say I know that God loves me, but I cannot know this without a doubt, because there are too many other possible explanations that might account for my claim to know it. Third, the kind of relativism that the postmodern stance often promotes is a kind that suggests there is no such thing as an authentic search for truth. Such a view often devolves into a search for the loudest voice as each side attempts to defend its own position. To say we lack certainty is in no way to deny the importance of treating one another with respect and does not mean that the honest and fair assessment of different points of view is either irrelevant or unnecessary.

Recognizing that theological claims are tradition-specific helps to make clear a second reason we should recognize the uncertainty that inevitably goes with theological claims: the nature of God as traditionally understood within the Christian context. Numerous arguments in the Christian tradition point in the direction of our inability to be certain of the truth of our claims about God. These arguments focus on such problems as the imperfection of human knowing, the imprecision of human language, distinctions between the nature and the actions of God, and the broad consensus that God's ways are not always the same as human ways. The emphasis through all of these is that claiming we know for sure what God is doing is the height of human pride and arrogance.

Does this mean that all theology (or, worse, everything at all) is simply a matter of opinion? No, not in the sense in which we usually mean this. Typically, when we claim that something is a matter of opinion, we mean that we cannot find convincing reasons to accept it or reject it but that, instead, personal preference or inclination appears to be the relevant and deciding factor. An important thrust of this book is that some views of God and God's relationship with the world are indeed better than others; even if we cannot know with certainty which corresponds most fully to Reality, we still may have very good reasons for choosing one view over the other. I point in later chapters to an approach for making such judgments.

Along with the philosophical and theological reasons for doubting that we can have certainty when seeking the ways of God, I also doubt this for two major empirical reasons. First, any inclination I might have for claiming some kind of certainty about God is challenged by the fact that Christian people of impressive intellect, deep spiritual awareness, and general goodwill believe many different things. Some say the Holy Spirit proceeds from the Father alone; others say from the Father and the Son. Some say "Father" is revealed language and a revealed concept about God; others say it is inappropriately exclusive and should at least be supplemented, in worship and elsewhere, with feminine imagery such as "Mother." Some say the Bible is literally God's word; others say the Bible is a collection of human experiences described in God-language. Christians disagree about who can legitimately call herself or himself a Christian and about which of them are saved and how. Some believe Christ is the only way to salvation; some believe there are many ways and that some of these can be found in the other great faith traditions of the world. Some wonder whether "salvation" is even the right concept for the end we seek. Some Christians take these differences of belief to be a matter of healthy diversity; others are sure that the long-term integrity of the church depends upon the right versions coming out on top in the historical free-for-all of doctrinal conversation. I have yet to discern any clear way to know with certainty what is the correct position on most of these issues on which various Christians stake their lives.

In addition, in churches and homes and stadiums around the world, we Christians regularly offer prayers, sing hymns, and recite creeds that presuppose the kinds of beliefs just mentioned. Some of us believe exactly what we say. Some of us have no understanding of what we are saying. Some of us see ourselves as articulating the value of a certain set of symbols or metaphors. Some of us are very selective as to the parts of prayers and hymns and creeds we affirm. Some of us suspend personal judgment in favor of the authority of our particular tradition or local community. Some of us suspend judgment in favor of the value of participation in a community of faith. Some of us have an aesthetic or moral appreciation for the whole of the tradition, though we cannot buy most of its details. And some of us have become so uncomfortable with what we are asked to affirm with our voices and actions in congregational worship, or in Christianity in general, that we are essentially alienated from the traditions of the church and are looking elsewhere for spiritual sustenance, without surrendering appreciation for or even adherence to the way of Jesus. The bottom line is that we are all looking for what we can say or do with meaning and integrity: for some of us, one or another version of Christianity works as it is; for others of us, no version we have encountered can claim our allegiance.

Personally, I am increasingly uncomfortable just saying or singing or reciting without being committed to, or sometimes without even believing, the words I am saying. To join the community at worship and yet not share the assumptions being made or the points of view being articulated in common parts of worship is sometimes alienating for me. In some sense, this discomfort is exactly right, because I *should* have a hard time affirming things about which I have serious doubts. While it is characteristic of me to try to find ways to work within systems that are, as all human systems are, in some ways harmful to the individual, as well as to work with individuals who are in some ways harmful to our institutions, I struggle with affirming things of faith that I cannot believe or to which I am not committed. I struggle with uncertainty.

I am not alone in my disorientation. Even as some people are finding a new home in various Christian communities, the popularity of books by authors such as John Shelby Spong, Marcus Borg, and others suggests to me that many who call themselves Christians are trying to find new ways to understand their faith in the midst of old ways that are not working for them. I speak to many who are unable to find a way of thinking about God and living out their faith that is not highly secularized—that is, a way that includes God only as a name and not as a reality—as well as many whose participation in Christian life is because of its communal value or the goodwill and good works of certain of its institutions. These are fine reasons to be associated with the tradition, but they ignore its vast and meaningful resources for making sense of our overall life journey. They ignore its history and power as a faith tradition.

As human beings and as Christians, we all live not only with epistemological uncertainty, but also with existential uncertainty. One aspect of this is my second major empirical reason for doubting the possibility of certainty with respect to the nature and ways of God. In general, we do not know what tomorrow will bring; we do not know whether joy or sorrow will fill the night ahead. We are never sure which minute we will be healthy and which minute we will be sick or injured; we cannot tell whether the next phone call will bring us joyful news or devastating news. This lack of certainty about the next moments of our existence would be less disconcerting were it not for the power of suffering.

All of us, at some point and in some way, suffer. Human beings have long wrestled with the implications of this fact. Put intellectually, the problem is how there can be such suffering in the world if God both loves us and can stop it. This problem has several possible solutions, including human freedom, the parental nature of God, reinterpretations of the meaning of God's love or God's power, but none of this, to my mind, successfully addresses the problem. Not only do such responses not account for either the breadth or the depth of human suffering, they do not account for God's obvious responsibility for this suffering if we take traditional conceptions seriously. If God could have created any world God wanted to create, and if God knows all and can see what we consider to be the future, then God willingly chose to create this world in which suffering is so prevalent. How do we make sense of the world within a tradition that offers us such a God?

In the midst of both intellectual and existential uncertainty, you and I must live and live well. In addition, if we accept the part of the Christian tradition that calls upon each one of us to love God not only with our heart and soul and strength, but also with our mind, we must strive to think well. Thinking well as theologians and living well as Christians are the ends to which this book points.

Theological Construction

Finally, it is worth introducing briefly the concept of theological construction. I believe I first saw this expression in Gordon Kaufman's *In Face of Mystery*.[1] All I mean by the phrase is the intentional human project of building a theological vision, a set of theological claims and images, to which we, as individuals in community, can commit ourselves. Theological construction, in this sense, is an attitude toward theological work, an attitude that rejects any uncritical acceptance of theological positions, whether these are supported with appeal to revelation, to the authority of the church or the Bible, or to familial or denominational tradition or affiliation. Theological construction highlights the importance of human intentionality in theological ideas and religious practices.

Intentional theological construction is the direct and appropriate consequence of our uncertainty. Confronted with epistemological and existential uncertainty about the ways of God (if there is a God), the meanings of our lives, and our next moment, our task is to employ all the rational and imaginative powers at our disposal to examine our traditions, our experiences, and ourselves with as much awareness as possible and to commit ourselves to what we can discern and test to be most true. The highest and best human ideals and constructions are the closest we can come to describing who God must be.

Putting our task in this way is not meant to suggest that I think we can separate ourselves from all the traditions that have made us who we are and start from zero to develop a theological perspective. I do not think this and do not intend to attempt it. Construction is neither *ex nihilo* (out of nothing) nor without accountability. I note up front the way in which the provisional character of all Christian subtraditions, not to mention of Christianity itself, should shape our theological reflections, namely by asking us to articulate our presuppositions and assumptions as best we can and to provide good reasons for the ideas and practices we accept. This is a never-ending process, one for which each Christian and each new generation is responsible.

My sense is that some would accuse me at this point of rejecting the revelatory heart of Christian faith. I do not see it that way. Instead, my intention is fourfold. I would like to encourage in a broad spectrum of Christians the intellectual love of God. I would like to inspire Christian commitment in the face of life's epistemological and existential uncertainties. I would like to show the hopefulness of Christian theological work. And I would like to offer a way for Christians and other interested people to think about and to live out their calling to love in daily life. It is likely that many of any given Christian person's faith positions will still remain through the process of critique and evaluation in which we are about to engage, but they will remain out of consciously and passionately chosen commitment and not out of uncritical acceptance. Why this will be better for all of us should become clear as the book proceeds.

Questions for Reflection

1. Have you been aware in your own life of the struggle I describe between living as a Christian and not being able to know for sure who God is and what God is doing? If so, how have you handled this struggle in the past?

2. If you have not taken the opportunity to write a sketch of your life and the changes in your faith, do so now. What have been the most important events in your life—good and bad? Have they in any way shaped your view of God? What has shaped your view?

3. Can you identify in your own life any points of contact with my life story? If we could sit down and talk, where might we find things in common and where would we not? Is this theologically significant?

4. Do you agree or disagree that it is important for each one of us to develop a personal theological point of view? Why?

5. How would you describe your theological or religious views at this point in your life? Who or what is God for you? Why? What do you think about the Bible? Jesus? Mary? Where have these ideas come from in your life, and why have you chosen to accept or reject them?

The following questions are based on the "Going Deeper" section of this chapter.

6. What is your evaluation of my claims about knowing? How are epistemological questions relevant to virtually every human pursuit?

7. How do you understand the differences between revelation and construction as theological tools, and how would you choose between them as a method for thinking about God?

8. Do you and I mean the same thing by the term "Christian"; if not, who is right and why? Why is this an important issue in today's political and religious climate?

2

Defining Faith and Theology

I am a person of faith. So are you. As human beings, the question is not whether we have faith, but what we have faith *in*. Some of us place our faith in some version of a "higher power," Christian or otherwise. Some of us have faith in friends and family, or in our bank accounts, or in ourselves, or in the power of reason to illuminate the world. It will help us to understand the most important parts of this chapter, on Christian faith and Christian theology, if we reflect first on faith more generally.

Faith, as a human way of making sense of and living in the world, is best understood in the context of three dimensions of the human condition. Every day, each one of us faces the existential and epistemological uncertainty about which I wrote in the previous chapter; this is the first important dimension. Second, we face the opportunity and, indeed, the necessity of making decisions about the directions of our lives. Third, we have what I call a hunger for the good life. We are not aware of these things most of the time, and, even when we are aware of them, we typically do not stop to ponder them. Yet they give shape to every moment of our lives in some way or another.

Making Choices

The greatest difficulty in living with uncertainty, as we all must do, is being forced to exercise our freedom in its midst. To be a human being is, in part, to make choices. It is to make significant and insignificant decisions virtually every minute of every day. We make these choices without knowing for sure their consequences and, therefore, without knowing for sure the conditions under which we will be choosing next. We choose one class to take without being certain whether another class would have had a more profound effect on us. We eat one kind of food rather than another without complete knowledge of its impact on our bodies and our health. We choose a career path without knowing whether another path will look better or worse retrospectively in twenty years. We marry without certainty about what that relationship will look like down the road, or we choose not to marry without any guarantees that our life will be better without a spouse. And, in the midst of all of our attempts to see clearly and to choose well, we do not know when the phone might ring in the middle of the night and change virtually everything we thought was true about the world. We do not know when a medical condition might appear that makes impossible the path on which we had settled or when a long-term illness might be cured and new possibilities opened to us. We do not know when the economic conditions of the place in which we live will change in a way that raises or shatters our hopes.

Each one of the choices we make alters the world and affects who we are. Some choices are likely to have a huge impact, as when the president decides to send soldiers to war or when you decide what job to take. Others will probably have very little impact, as when you decide which brand of toothpaste to buy. Each choice, however, is a part of the creation of a different world than would have otherwise been the case and sets us up with different choices ahead than we would have had in following a different path; each choice sets us on a different trajectory through life. I suspect it is a good thing that we do not notice this implication of our choosing, or we might face crises about our decision making far more often than we do now. In pondering what it means to be a human being, though, it is worth bringing to our consciousness from time to time the fact that each choice, however small, defines us as a particular human being and makes some kind of difference in the world, in many cases for better or for worse.

If this seems exaggerated, or even ridiculous, pause where you are right now and run through a brief exercise in your head. Notice the vast number of choices you have in this moment, most of them choices that would not have occurred to you had you not been invited to ponder them. Typically, we do not reflect on our possible choices moment by moment; we set our course for the day or the year and aim toward our defined end. This obliviousness probably helps us to stay sane, but it also narrows the life we will have.

Consider this: Currently, I am sitting in my office at Hanover College at about 10:30 on a Monday morning, writing on a Macintosh computer, sipping from a mug of Jamoca Almond Fudge coffee from time to time, and starting to get hungry for lunch. What choices might I make at this moment and what would their consequences be? I have here, waiting for an answer, an invitation from a friend to get together for lunch in Louisville in the next couple of weeks. I might respond now or another time or never; I might respond affirmatively or negatively; in the end, I might drive the ninety-mile round-trip safely or never return. I might choose not to let myself be distracted from my writing by waiting e-mails or anything else right now. This might result in this book being finished more quickly, unless my computer crashes before I remember to print out what I have just written. I might decide that I am tired of drinking coffee, that the juice in my office refrigerator is better for me, and walk across the room in search of the more nutritious drink. In the process, I might well forget what I am thinking about and return to my writing with no sense of what I was saying. I might tire of writing, pick up the daily paper on my other desk, and read it. Whatever I find there will add to the information I have and the choices I might make; there will be people in crisis whom I might help, sporting and theater events I might attend, letters and editorials to which I might respond. Any of these could alter my life and the lives of others in numerous ways. I might pause in my writing to pay a couple of bills or make a donation to charity, to go for a walk on this beautiful spring day, to talk with a colleague in the office next door to me. I might finish writing a letter to my father for Father's Day. Instead of any immediate actions, I might simply contemplate why so many folks in the world are not able to eat lunch today and what I can do about that, given that I am probably going to head to my favorite café in an hour and spend ten dollars on lunch. I might sit back and ponder what I will get my girlfriend for our second anniversary "if we do well" (her favorite expression). I might reflect back on a conversation I had with a marathon runner a few weeks ago and decide to go to the gym for a workout. And all of the things that I might do or think would actually have some influence on the shape of the world around me and on my own identity, if only in the sense that a state of affairs would be brought about that had not previously existed; some changes could be much more significant, depending in part on others' responses to what I do. This is our situation as human beings. We must choose, but we are always in a position where all we can do is to take our best shot at this thing called life; we cannot know for sure what our choices will bring. If you have not yet tried the exercise, I invite you to do so before continuing to read. Give yourself as full a sense as possible of the situation you are in as a free human being, even if you generally do not ponder the question.

⊸◇⊸◇⊸◇⊸◇⊸◇⊸◇⊸◇⊸

While it is important to recognize the choices we all face minute by minute, not all choices are equally good and not all choices we can imagine are actually possible. Of all the choices we have in any given moment, only some of them will be worth making. Only some of them will contribute to the world rather than detract from it. In any given moment, I may be able to choose to harm someone, for instance, but that does not mean that this would be a good or right choice to make. In many cases, even seeing certain actions as choices will go against our characters. For instance, I have to stretch even to see that I could possibly choose to wander to the next office and kick my colleague in the ankle. On the whole, the way our character has been formed makes some choices virtually impossible for us, and that is probably a very good thing, for it means our willpower will not have to be tested any more frequently than it already is.

Further, in real situations, we choose within parameters. For example, there is no meaningful sense in which I can choose at this moment to go and buy a yacht; my financial condition prohibits this, just as my physical condition prohibits me from choosing to participate in Olympic trials in pole vaulting. To note my many choices is different from looking into a Wal-Mart store with a hundred dollars in my hand, thereby having an almost unlimited number of things I might purchase. There are constraints of many kinds—economic, genetic, moral, psychological—on the actual choices I have in a given moment. Regardless of how many constraints there may be, however, I must choose between them, and I must do so without certainty about the consequences.

In this human context of uncertainty and necessary choice (two of the three dimensions of human life essential for understanding faith), the metaphors of invitation or interrogation, or even demand, are helpful. Without going so far, yet, as to give personality to the universe or say anything about the workings of God, we can see, metaphorically, that the universe poses a question to each conscious person in each moment. The question is always the same: how will you respond to this place, this moment, these conditions? Put another way, what kind of person do you wish to be, or what will you make of the world in this moment? These latter two questions, however close they may be to the original, may actually suggest a greater degree of influence on the future than we have (since I cannot, for instance, be an Olympic pole vaulter), but the point is the same: *the universe demands that we choose*.

Seeking the Good Life

What guides these choices we must make? As human beings, we all strive to make sense of our world, to find meaning in life or to give meaning to life. We ponder what we are to do with our lives, wonder why we must die, work hard to decide what is right and what is wrong. At some point and in some way, each one of us tries to make sense of such mysteries as why we act the way we do, why there is anything instead of nothing, and how to relate to others. That is, we desire not simply to live, but to live well. We try to account for our lot in life, and, given where and who we are, we want to do the best we can. This desire to live well is the third dimension of human life that can help us to understand the nature and work of faith.

You may object that it is only the comparatively wealthy in history and in the world today who have the leisure to ponder these things. A book such as Jonathan Kozol's *Amazing Grace*, in which underprivileged children in the South Bronx reflect on some of these very issues, suggests that these concerns are not only those of the wealthy.[1] It certainly is the case, however, that some people have greater opportunities than others to make such pondering a relatively large portion of their lives and that a few have greater opportunity than most to act on the results of their thinking. This simply means that some of us have a greater responsibility for the well-being of the world. For our purposes here, it is enough to realize that there is something deep within human beings that prompts us to seek to live well, even though the particular shape of our seeking and the particular meaning we give to the good life will vary considerably depending upon our life context.

Clearly, the expression "living well," and such related notions as living the good life, living a fulfilling life, living a happy life, and living a life that one can affirm, are relative terms in the sense that human beings do not agree on the standard against which they should be measured. To give an example, collecting rare books, even to the limited extent that my financial condition makes possible, makes me happy. I enjoy the feel and smell and contents of an eighteenth-century *Book of Common Prayer* or a first edition *Hound of the Baskervilles.* Many of my friends are interested enough in me or gracious enough to me to listen as I talk about this hobby, but they cannot personally imagine why anyone would be interested in a pile of old, dusty pieces of paper. Collecting rare books would bore some of them, others prefer other ways of spending their money, and still others would find the expense unconscionable. Some might even accuse me of poor stewardship, as one did recently. (I argued that it is actually good stewardship to preserve rare volumes for future generations, but this does not fully meet the objection some might make that my view of the good life is rather odd.)

One way to deal with different understandings of what it means to live well is to make our standards relative to individuals. Thus, each one of us sets her or his own standard for living the good life. If, then, collecting rarities makes me happy and if I do not mind spending my money that way instead of giving it to those who are in greater need than I am, then that is my business and you should stop bothering me and go find something that makes you happy. However, this view is unsatisfactory on at least three grounds. Although each of them is much more complex than it would be useful to explore here, it is worth pointing to them briefly. First, most human beings do not actually believe that this kind of individualism is true. We do not believe that each person has or should have the unlimited freedom to define the good life in any way he or she sees fit and to act on that. We do not believe, for instance, that the person next to me, who wishes to define the good life as the life where he gets to punch me in the mouth whenever he feels like it, should be allowed to live out his vision. Typically, we do not think he is right about thinking that this is the good life; even if he is, we think he should be stopped from living it out because it is likely to work against his neighbor's vision of the good life. This may be both a moral and a logical objection.

Second, even if living out your vision of the good life does not interfere with living out my vision, you are likely to believe that I am not living well if I am acting in ways that are harmful to myself. Although what counts as harmful will vary from culture to culture and from age to age, we have all seen the negative effects that too much stress, alcohol addiction, or promiscuity can have. We understand that too much of some things (and too little of other things, such as food or love) impedes the pursuit of any good life we judge to be appropriate. I encourage you to ponder what it means if we can identify shared conditions and behaviors that contribute to the optimal functioning of human beings as well as conditions and behaviors that impede full human living. What would the implications of these perceptions be for the notion that the good life should be judged according to individual standards?

The third reason the individual standard is unsatisfactory stems from the ultimate context of this book: the Christian perspective. However we wish to define what it means to be a Christian, the notion that all of us are to love our neighbors and ourselves is an important part of the Christian attitude toward the world. Even if there were no other standards offered by the Christian tradition, this one would be sufficient to rule out many of the possible implications of permitting unlimited individual standards of the good life.

In the next chapter, I return to the question of how we should assess various ways of living. For now, it is sufficient to have in mind that all of us seek to make sense of our lives, which includes trying to discover or articulate what it means to live well. This is the third dimension of the human condition that, along with the dimensions of uncertainty and the necessity of choosing, provides the context for coming to understand faith. Putting the dimensions together, we can say that our task as human beings is to live well in the midst of the universe's apparent requirement that we exercise our power of free choice without certainty about the consequences of our choices, the implications of our choices for the next choice we will have to make, or what the world will present to us in the next moment.

Fortunately, we are not without help in facing our task. Lessons from our parents guide us in what to do or in what not to do. Literature provides us with models of lives we might live. Sacred texts offer guidance on the good life and on what we will face as we seek to live it. The rationality that is a basic characteristic of being human helps us to sort out causes and likely effects. Faith is the tool that underlies all of these. Without faith it would be incoherent and unhelpful to rely upon any of them.

Living by Faith

At the heart of this book is my invitation to you to explore your own faith convictions and to construct your own personal theological view. I am about to present my understanding of what it means to live by faith. I have spent months pondering what you are about to read and have explored many definitions of faith. You may know the biblical definition from Hebrews 11:1: "the assurance of things hoped for, the conviction of things not seen." You may have read Reformation theologian John Calvin's view of faith as "a firm and certain knowledge of God's benevolence toward us, founded upon the truth of the freely given promise in Christ, both revealed to our minds and sealed upon our hearts through the Holy Spirit."[2] You probably have not seen, but might want to reflect upon philosopher William Alston's characterization of faith as "trusting whatever we do have to go on as providing us with a picture of the situation that is close enough to the truth to be a reliable guide to our ultimate destiny."[3] Before you continue, pause in your reading and consider how you would describe faith. Does one of the above characterizations seem right to you? What would you add to them or take away from them so that they reflect your understanding of faith? Some initial thoughts of your own will be of enormous help to you as you sort out where you stand on the theological questions we address later.

<hr />

If you have pondered your view of faith, you are in a position to see where you and I are thinking differently and where we are thinking similarly on this important issue. My view is this: To live by faith, as we all do, is to rely in our living upon a set of articulable but frequently unarticulated and unconscious ways of seeing the world and our place in it. It is to depend, in virtually every moment, upon the truth of these ways of seeing, these deep and enduring assumptions or convictions, for they provide us with the personal resources necessary for facing successfully the uncertain world. Were our fundamental assumptions about our place in the world to disappear suddenly, we would find it difficult, if not impossible, to take another step. Put simply, I sometimes say that our faith enables us to get out of bed in the morning; occasionally, that becomes a reality instead of a metaphor. To use a different metaphor, our deepest assumptions are the rocks on which we stand, and it can take an earthquake to make us give them up or alter them significantly. Indeed, it can occasionally take an earthquake to bring these deep convictions to our awareness.

Our deepest convictions provide us with such resources as courage, strength, hope, a sense of security or safety, a sense of being okay, and a sense of having a place in the world or being at home in the world. This is not to say that well-formed deep convictions will guarantee that we never feel scared, hopeless, or alienated from the world. After all, the world can be a scary place sometimes. Furthermore, convictions that lead us to miss real threats are not well formed. Also, some of our faith convictions may entail such heart-wrenching things as standing by and watching while our children make significant mistakes, knowing that not interfering will be better for them in the long run of life. The point of faith convictions is to enable us to live well, which typically will not include being immobilized with fear or hopelessness, but which may well mean making hard choices that cause pain or suffering to others or to us. The situations in which we are raised, our genetic makeup, and the choices we make are all involved in the continual forming, shaping, and reshaping of the faith convictions and assumptions that guide us through life.

As this book continues, we will examine a number of faith convictions. It is worth noting, therefore, that a person's faith convictions are not always easy to identify, for at least two reasons. The first reason is that we typically observe persons' behaviors, and any given behavior is consistent with many different assumptions. For instance, if I see you walk into a church building on Sunday morning, I would probably not know whether you are a pastor who has no religious faith but has a deep conviction that says he is responsible for feeding his family. I would typically not know whether you are driven by an assumption that churches provide fellowship, even though you do not believe any of the doctrines they promote. I would not know whether you believe with your whole heart that your church and only your church offers the way of salvation for all people. Your action of walking into the church on Sunday morning is consistent with any of these assumptions and with many others.

The second reason faith convictions are difficult to identify is closely related to the first: we express them in a wide variety of ways. We may paint or exhibit a photograph or write a poem or have a family picnic or take a particular job; any one of these might be an expression of one of our deep faith convictions. In this book, we look most closely at faith's articulation in linguistic expressions such as "My family will never let me down," "I can handle anything life throws at me," "God loves the world," and "Money is the source of all happiness." It is always worth asking whether paintings or giving money to charity actually expresses a given conviction or set of convictions better than the words with which one can attempt to describe it, but I remain convinced that virtually all of our faith convictions are linguistically accessible and expressible. Human language is the realm in which we will work in this book.

Watching Faith Change

One way to grasp the meaning and importance of having faith in this fundamental, human way is to watch carefully moments in life when one *loses* faith, or when one's faith is called into question. I said in the introductory chapter that I have experienced periodic bouts of anxiety and depression over the last several years, and I share here additional details of one of these bouts as a way to help us understand the role of faith in our lives. You should know that I am not sharing this example lightly. It is not easy to write, and more than one reader has found it difficult to read. However, I am convinced that these kinds of life-shaping times often teach us the most about ourselves and our faith convictions, so I am sharing this partly because it enables me to highlight my own convictions most clearly, and partly as an encouragement to you to listen for what your own life has taught you in good times and in bad. Such listening is often best done in multiple sittings and in conversation with trusted friends or counselors.

My first bout with anxiety and depression started one day in late 2001 as I was driving to New England to visit my father and sister for Christmas. Along the way, I started to feel a deep desperation, accompanied by an intense, full-body anxiety. I spent only one night at my father's house, leaving quickly to get back on more familiar ground, hoping that this would help. It did not. I began almost-daily meetings with a counselor, who sometimes had to come to my home and who talked with me from time to time about the possibility of hospitalization. I started taking the antidepressant medication Zoloft and called a friend in Virginia who graciously came and stayed with me for a week. I felt completely hopeless and helpless and was afraid I was going to die, perhaps by my own hand.

The darkest time lasted for a month, and my despair became almost absolute. I have a sense of myself running—running to get out of the house in the morning, running from person to person and conversation to conversation—trying to find relief from the anxiety, the hopelessness, the terror that filled each moment. I remember thinking that I just was not able to live in this world, that some organisms cannot survive and that I was one of them. At the same time that I wanted to run, of course, I also wanted to curl up in a ball and shut out the world.

The emotional pressure of this time eroded my sense of being able to face the world. Had you asked me, in those days, to articulate my deepest faith convictions, I would have said I had none. Or, perhaps, I would have said that any ones I had were inoperable, did not work, were not ones I could rely on to get me through. The love on which I used to rely in hard times—my mother's, my wife's, God's—was gone, the first because my mother was long dead, the second because I was divorced, the third because God was not answering. The sense of God's presence that had so often been with me in life was gone, and my convictions about God's reality began to die as well. Prayer, when I could actually focus enough to do it, had no noticeable consequences. In the end, the only thing that enabled me to survive this time was the persistent and patient love of family and friends on the telephone and by my side. As they moved me beyond the one-month mark, there began to be a few minutes, then an hour, then a few hours, when the anxiety subsided and hope began to dawn that I would feel normal again. As another month passed, it gradually became a bit easier to put one foot in front of the other and, miraculously, the time arrived when I awoke to an anxiety-free day. I did, indeed, come to feel normal again.

I share this with you in order to illuminate what it means to have faith by showing what it means to lose faith. We all have faith. We all live by faith. Sometimes, we lose pieces of the faith we have. For me, the changes in my faith—my reliance on certain convictions to enable me to live well—during those two months of struggle were so deep that I am still not clear how to express them correctly. As I see it today, there were two crucial assumptions I relied upon that I learned I could rely upon no longer: first, important people in my life would be in my life forever, providing me with the energy and the reason to live; second, I would always be able to experience God in a direct one-to-one relationship. Had I actually articulated these, I would have been quick to point to the impossibility of defending them intellectually, for I had seen many things in my life and in the lives of others that had called them into question. Still, deeper layers of them than I had yet questioned were among the many assumptions on which I relied to attempt to navigate my way through life successfully and well. I now had the most powerful evidence yet of their inadequacy.

Even with the onset of my mother's illness in my childhood, the death of all of my grandparents, and the ending of a couple of significant romantic relationships, I continued to look to my mother and, eventually, my wife for some meaningful amount of my life definition. Upon reflection, it seems to me that I simply wanted them to be proud of me, but I have no doubt that this manifested itself in ways that were not emotionally healthy. Both my mother and my wife were long gone at the time of my first major bout with anxiety and depression, and my experience was partly the recognition that they were no longer in my life and partly a prompt to find my life energy from within myself rather than in significant others. One basic conviction of my life had to die.

God was also dead during this time; at least that was my experience. You will see here, as I do, the connection in my heart between the significant human presences in my life and my ability to sense God, but all I felt at the time was absence, including God's absence. I had no illusion that God protects us from horrible times, or even from death, in any certain, consistent, and material way. But I had always relied on my occasional "mountaintop" experiences of God and my ability to sense their relevance to the current moment—to sense God in the current moment, it seemed—to carry me through difficult times. All of this seemed like an illusion in my darkest time. If there was any God, and I frequently doubted this, then God appeared to be irrelevant to me and to my pain. In my experience, God was as dead as my mother and as distant from me as my wife now had to be.

One way to understand the change in me that occurred as a part of this crisis of faith would be to say that it forced upon me a reconstruction of my faith. Before the crisis, my convictions centered upon God and myself in direct, one-on-one relationship, as modeled by and emotionally inspired by my energy-providing relationships with certain significant female others. Today, with my crisis behind me, my convictions are centered more on my broad relationships with others as expressions of God's working in the world. I have always understood myself to be part of a community, but my clarity about the reality and the power of that community has been deepened in these last several years, to the point that the community that surrounds me with care has become, in actuality even if not in theory, more important to me than the workings of the individually oriented spirituality with which I previously lived. This is oversimplified, but it illustrates what it means to lose faith convictions or to have them change. It should also illustrate what it means to have faith in the first place.

My example above shows the nonreligious quality of some of our most deeply held convictions, even though it also shows that one of mine was a religious conviction. Were we to list the basic convictions of each person, I expect we would find many fundamental convictions shared by most human beings as well as more individualized convictions stemming from such things as a given person's upbringing, geography, and social location. Were we to put the whole collection of faith assumptions into categories, we would find both broad and general religious convictions as well as convictions related to particular religious traditions. To say it again, all persons are persons of faith; only some of these persons are persons of *religious* faith, that is, persons who hold basic convictions that are best articulated in terms of various sacred authorities. These typically fit into a subset associated with one of the major world religious traditions, such as Buddhism, Hinduism, or Islam, but may also be a comparatively unique and composite grouping that has been internalized, consciously or unconsciously, by just one given individual. Given the focus of this book on Christian faith and Christian theology, our next task is to try to identify what it is that makes a person's basic convictions Christian as opposed to non-Christian. At that point, we will be ready to discuss the nature of theology.

What Is Christian Faith? What Is Christian Theology?

We have done sufficient groundwork to make describing Christian faith and theology a fairly easy task. I wrote in the first chapter that "this book is addressed to those who somehow put Jesus of Nazareth at the center of their spiritual life. . . ." Although I did not define the term "spiritual" there, I am using the word to point to the divine-human relationship. Christians, then, take Jesus to be central for their understanding of and relationship with God, and this relationship makes a difference in their thinking and living.

In the heart and mind of any given Christian person, as well as at the center of the life of any given Christian community, there are a wide variety of specific convictions or assumptions that accompany this basic one concerning the centrality of Jesus. Some of these will be spoken aloud, as in Christian worship when one of the traditional creeds is said on a Sunday morning: "I believe in God, the Father almighty, Creator of heaven and earth. I believe in Jesus Christ, God's only Son, our Lord. . . . He will come again to judge the living and the dead. I believe in the Holy Spirit . . . the resurrection of the body, and the life everlasting."[4] Other convictions we hold will not frequently be verbalized, but, instead, can be seen in the behavior of Christian people. A man lays down his life for his friends. Another person becomes a peacemaker. A woman brings hope to her neighbors. Someone visits the sick, feeds the hungry, and clothes the poor. As suggested earlier, it can take careful analysis to discern the convictions behind whatever a Christian person says or does; after all, one does not have to be a Christian to act in any of the ways just mentioned.

Putting together everything we have said, *Christian faith is reliance upon a set of articulable but frequently unarticulated and unconscious assumptions or convictions that, taken together, demonstrate the centrality of Jesus to a person's relationship with God and provide her or him with resources to live well in an uncertain world.* Of course, Christians also rely in their living upon faith convictions that have no particular religious content, but it is likely that many of their most enduring and influential ones reflect the importance of Jesus and God for them. Christian faith convictions, those that do have Christian content or are so connected to these as to be almost as important in a person's life, are the raw material for Christian theology. At its simplest, then, Christian theology is thinking about Christian faith. More adequately, the task of Christian theology is to notice, articulate, analyze, assess, and either accept or reject the faith assumptions of Christians, a person's or community's reliance upon them, the resources for living well that they provide, and the actions that flow from them and from reliance upon them. Of course, parallel statements can be made with respect to other religious traditions, and analogous statements can be made for nonreligious traditions or individual orientations, but our focus is on the faith and lives of Christians.

How Are Faith and Theology Related?

In my two decades of teaching, I have found that students commonly dread theology classes, on one of two grounds. Some students think theology is about telling people what they should believe in matters of faith, and they have had enough of that already. Others think theology is about destroying faith and enter classes with the attitude that they know what they believe and no one is going to change their minds. I hope that, as students take theology classes, they realize that theology is neither about telling people what to believe nor about destroying faith. These confusions, though, make it important to say something more about the relationship between faith and theology. I hope this will also serve to relieve any worries you may have that this book is either an extended sermon meant to tell you what to believe or a subtle manipulation meant to lead you to deny your faith. It is neither of these. I am an advocate for a strong Christian faith and believe that this is most possible through a rigorous theological exploration of our deepest convictions. Here, I want to acquaint you with theological tools for making decisions about where you stand on matters of Christian faith as you face this exciting but uncertain world in which we all live. Following are three examples meant to highlight the relationship between theology and faith in a Christian context.

Although I have been a Protestant Christian all my life, I have sometimes found solace and other connection with God in the practices of Roman Catholic Christianity. So it was that, during a personal retreat several years ago, I was walking through a Roman Catholic church, pausing to pray before its Stations of the Cross. A few Stations along the path, I noticed movement in the balcony above me. A nun was seated there, saying the Rosary. Her head was slightly bowed, her eyes appeared to be closed, and her fingers were gliding along the beads. I watched her for a moment and then tried to say the words of the Hail Mary at the pace at which she was moving her hands. "Hail Mary, full of grace, the Lord is with thee. . . ."[5] She was on to the next bead long before I could articulate even the first few words.

I returned to my own prayers and never met this nun, but I am going to assume for purposes of this discussion that saying the Rosary was, for her, a practice that expressed her deep Christian commitment. This practice had become so much a part of her that she did not need to focus on each word of the Hail Mary as she moved from bead to bead; rather, the words and movements focused her. Through them she touched the presence and activity of Mary, Christ, and God. This communion with what was in some sense beyond her and in some sense within her granted to her a sense of well-being in the midst of whatever possibilities and challenges the day and the world might bring. Those moments on the balcony both expressed and strengthened her fundamental orientation to life.

I do not know whether this nun had either the time or the inclination to do much intentional theological reflection, but her practice of the Rosary is a testimony to the investment others have made in that adventure through the centuries. The practice depends upon a number of discussions and decisions made over the centuries concerning issues such as the importance of Mary to the Christian life, who Mary is (full of grace, for example), her relationship to Christ and to God, and whether she can pray for us in some particularly efficacious way. Each claim that might be made concerning one of these issues represents a deep conviction or a set of convictions to which this nun and other Christians subscribe, but which they may or may not have critiqued in a systematic way. These claims are part of the system that has been developed through discussion, debate, conflicts, and riots over the centuries and which helps some Christians to navigate the world successfully and to carry a sense of belonging and hope with them in its midst. These convictions have emerged historically from the critical process known as theology, and theology continues to articulate and examine them, not with a predetermined intent to deny or affirm them, but to wrestle honestly with whether or not they contribute to or detract from a full and good life.

Here is another example of theology at work. Until recently, I regularly taught an introductory theology course entitled "Theology and Images of God." At the beginning of that course, I usually passed out copies of the Lord's Prayer, a prayer said weekly by Christians around the world, a prayer that, arguably, binds them to their ancestors in faith and sustains their daily living. Most of the students in the class have seen the prayer before and many of them say it regularly, but their familiarity with it or commitment to its meanings have little bearing on their ability to think about what it is saying. To help the students begin to ponder the various ways Christians imagine God to be, I ask them to name the ways of understanding God that are in the words of the prayer. In the first line, we usually find the ideas that God is Father, that God is "our" Father and not just the Father of one of us, and that God is in heaven. We then begin to discuss what these claims might mean. Consider these questions yourself. What does it mean to say that God is a Father, and in what ways might God be like or unlike a human father? What are the implications for human relationships of saying that God is "our" corporate Father? What does it mean to talk about heaven, what might heaven be like, and why might anyone believe in it? What does it mean to say that God is there, in heaven? Does that have any implications for whether God is here, with us? What might it mean to claim any of these beliefs as one's own? Would it make a difference in how one experienced the world or in how one lived? Why might or might not a given individual or community subscribe to these kinds of positions? These are all theological questions. That is, they are all questions intended to explore critically deep and frequently unarticulated and unassessed assumptions and convictions of faith (convictions that in this case lie behind a particular Christian prayer) with an eye to discerning the meaning of our lives and how we should live. They help us to ponder the quality and reality of the relationship we have to the world, other people, and the Other on whom we as Christians rely.

Consider a final example. Two or three years ago, I was at the Abbey of St. Meinrad's in southern Indiana for a few days of reflection. In the middle of one especially beautiful afternoon, I was sitting on a bench in a small wooded area thinking about life when I became aware of a powerful and comforting feeling that God was with me. I simply sat and rested in that feeling for a little while. Later, as I reflected back on those moments on the bench, several questions occurred to me: Was this feeling what I thought it was? Was God really with me? What made me think this feeling was caused by the presence of God instead of simply being a strong feeling of comfort caused, for example, by the peacefulness of the place where I was sitting? Does God speak to us through feelings? Does God speak to us at all?

Here is a theological analysis of my experience: I went to St. Meinrad's as a Christian, which means that my experiences there were bound to be shaped by the convictions I brought with me. This is likely to have affected what I experienced as well as how I experienced it. Another important fact to know about me is that I have typically felt close to God at monasteries and retreat centers. On this particular trip, I was trying to get a handle on some of the emotional and practical consequences of my divorce and was seeking to be centered in God as much as possible. On this afternoon, the woods where I was sitting were very peaceful and the day was very beautiful. Given these facts, one might say that I was predisposed to feel some comfort during these moments. The peacefulness of the setting was especially noticeable to me, given the soreness of my heart. Add to this heightened awareness of my surroundings my past experiences at similar places and my Christian understanding of the world, and thus it is reasonable that I would have an experience of comfort and that I would explain it as the presence of God. My life situation and my personal history provide some degree of insight into what I experienced in those moments on the bench and how I interpreted that experience.

Not everyone would have had the same experience in a similar situation. Someone who was already feeling at peace in his or her heart might not have noticed anything extra peaceful about those moments. Someone who does not believe there is a God might have had exactly the same feeling I had (at least, as close as two people can come to having the same feeling), but simply say that sitting on that bench in the cool breezes of those woods at that time on such a beautiful day was a very comforting thing. Someone of a different faith tradition might have had exactly the same feeling and name the One they believed was with them by a name other than "God." Another Christian might have the same feeling I had but say that Mary was present with them or, perhaps, that it always feels peaceful to them on the grounds of St. Meinrad's. Someone else might even have said that God is not a God of peace but a God of justice, and that I am deluding myself if I think God will give me comfort when (in this person's eyes) I have yet to repent of my sins.

Given all of these important questions and possible explanations of my experience, do I still want to claim that I rested in God's presence for a few wonderful moments that afternoon at the Abbey? Theology enables me to examine my convictions and to decide whether or not to retain them. It is the disciplined approach to the interpretation and assessment of Christian faith convictions that invites us into the depths of ourselves to discover and claim where we must stand in order to make sense of our lives as we seek to live well in an uncertain world. In the end, I freely admit that I can have no certainty about God's presence in those moments or about God's presence ever. However, I have yet to find another fundamental perspective on life that enables me to live as well as the perspective that includes the assumption that we sometimes sense God as or in feelings of peacefulness. We will soon see more fully what it means to test such convictions, but my testing to this point in my life says that I sensed God with me in those moments at St. Meinrad's.

Could I Be Wrong about All This?

Critical thinking, whether or not of the theological variety, demands honest critique of our own views as well as the views of others. In theology, where we are dealing with some of the most difficult and most important questions and issues with which human beings are faced, this is perhaps especially important. In this final section of the chapter, I want to respond to several objections that you may raise.

In every class I teach, someone argues that fundamental religious convictions are simply matters of opinion. When this is something other than an attempt to get out of the hard work of critical thinking, it appears to be a shorthand version of at least three separate objections to the theological enterprise. The first objection is that there is no way to determine the truth of such convictions. The objector here accepts the epistemological uncertainty with which we all live (as we discussed earlier), but takes an implication of this to be that, at least in religious matters, we cannot discuss what is true but only what our various opinions may be. This objection assumes what is sometimes called the correspondence theory of truth. On this view, theological statements are judged to be true or false according to their correspondence to reality. Thus, "God loves me" is true or false depending upon whether there really is a God and that God loves me. According to the objector, we cannot know for sure whether there is a God, so we cannot know whether "God loves me" is true or false.

I deny this view of truth. Epistemological uncertainty does not imply that everything is a matter of opinion; rather, it points to a different conception of truth than that of the correspondence theory. Rather than asking, using the example of Christian religious claims, whether they correspond with reality, the question to be asked is whether they fit within the parameters of appropriate Christian faith claims—the topic of the next chapter—and whether they work in enabling us to live well. Theologians are pragmatists who understand the limits of human certainty and do not pretend to measure faith convictions against that which is unknowable in any objective and certain way. Rather, such convictions as "God loves me" are to be examined to see whether they cohere with all of the Christian's conversation partners (as presented in the next chapter), such as Scripture and tradition, and whether they contribute to a life well lived for all people. If we can affirm them on these grounds, then we can affirm them as true. I could, in this case, truthfully say that God loves me.

A second objection that is sometimes intended by claiming that religious convictions are simply matters of opinion is that such convictions are so deeply personal that they are not subject to evaluation by anyone else. This is sometimes expressed in the statement, "I just know it's true, and I don't have to prove it to you." What I appreciate about this objection is the level of discernment it may reveal. The claim that "I just know" can indicate that a person is in touch with the place in himself or herself where his or her deepest convictions reside, which is a requirement of the autobiographical approach to theological exploration.

The two things I cannot accept in this objection, however, are giving in to the fear that it often reveals and accepting its individualistic implications. It can certainly be scary to examine one's convictions, and even scarier to put them before others for examination, but in the end this is the primary way that we can avoid self-deception and come to understand where we should really stand in life. Indeed, one of the strengths of the theological adventure as I am describing it here is its cooperative style: open-minded and openhearted exploration enables the clarification and strengthening of faith convictions, instead of the mere repetition of what others have handed to us. Admittedly, not all theologians are especially open-minded or openhearted, but theology at its best is, and these are virtues to which we are aspiring here.

The third objection that is sometimes intended is that it is pointless to debate issues on which we are never going to reach agreement. This objection appears to emerge out of an increasing recognition that there are almost as many versions of religious faith as there are religious people in the world. It also appears to reflect the general frustration many of us have at hearing conflicting voices on various social issues that try with political manipulation and loud voices to make up for lack of clear argument. People believe different things and they always will, the argument goes, so why fight about it? Why not live and let live? The answer, of course, is that there is no reason to fight about it, but there are good reasons to have respectful, informed, honest, and vigorous conversations. The reasons include deepened self-understanding, improved relationships with one another, and a better life for all of us as we discover those convictions upon which we can best rest our lives.

A final objection that may occur to you is that by making theological exploration about personal faith convictions, I have shifted the subject of theology from God to human beings. Is it not the work of the theologian to tell us about God and not just about ourselves? I do believe that there is an objective reality. Christians believe this at least as much as other human beings do. I walk through my doorway when I leave my office because I know it would hurt to try walking through my wall. The world is constructed in certain ways rather than others. There is something "out there" with which human beings interact. Thus, there *is* a right answer to the question of whether there is a God. There *are* right answers to the questions of whether heaven exists, prayer works, Jesus saves, and angels can dance on the heads of pins. I have no doubt about the existence of objective reality in this sense. The problem is that we do not have certain knowledge of this external reality. More accurately, we may know the answers to the questions I just raised, but *we cannot know that we know them.* Again, epistemological certainty is not available to human beings. Without such certainty, we need some way to assess the validity of claims about the world, so that we are not simply left with a series of statements such as "The streets of heaven are paved with gold," or "There is no salvation outside of the church," and no way to assess or evaluate them. And the standards for evaluation are communal and multiple and pragmatic, as the following chapter discusses.

But when all the assessment is through, each one of us stands alone before the universe. Others may support us, encourage us, sacrifice for us, but as we move toward adulthood, we are increasingly responsible for what we believe and how we act. Your community, family, pastor, friends, classmates, and teachers are not responsible for what you believe; you are. Nor are they responsible for how you act; you are. The faith convictions of the heart are not the subject matter of theology in the sense that they arise from nothing into our heart and mind. But they are accepted or rejected by each one of us, individually. No matter what claims other Christians may make, and no matter what authority we each give to those who make Christian claims or shape Christian lives, the convictions we each carry with us are ultimately our own responsibility. Sorting out, from among the nearly infinite possibilities, which convictions we accept and which ones we reject is the work of theology as we attempt to find our way in the world. This is true even if there is an objective reality out there, and even if, as I argue, the Christian aim is not just good life for us as individuals but good life for all of Creation as one.

To remind you, then, your task is to construct your own theological vision of the world. My task is to lead you through the steps of doing that. We have now built the foundation for this work by coming to see Christian faith as reliance upon a set of articulable assumptions or convictions that, taken together, express the centrality of Jesus to a person's relationship with God and that provide that person with resources to live well in this uncertain world. Such faith is made one's own through the work of Christian theology, which is the disciplined approach to the interpretation and assessment of Christian faith convictions that invites us into the depths of ourselves to discover and claim where we must stand in order to make sense of our lives as we seek to live well. That we are going to stand somewhere is certain; that we are going to stand in the best possible place is up to us.

Questions for Reflection

1. What do you think of the notion that everyone is a person of faith?

2. I name three dimensions of being a human being. Am I right? Is my list complete? Can you think of other dimensions that might change the way we think about ourselves and God?

3. What is your view of the good life? What about it makes it good?

4. How did you define faith? Why? In what ways, if any, is your definition different from mine?

5. Has your faith been important to you in the past? Would someone who watched you for twenty-four hours be able to say much about your faith?

6. Has your faith ever been seriously challenged? What did you learn about yourself, faith, and God during this time?

7. Are faith convictions matters of opinion? How would you argue in support of your point of view? What is your assessment of my view that faith convictions are not matters of opinion?

8. Can you put in your own words what faith and theology are and how they are related? Would you have said the same thing before reading the chapter?

3

Partners in Christian Conversations

Christian history might be imagined as an uncountable number of small and large clusters of Christian people living out their most closely held and most life-shaping convictions about themselves and their world. Over the centuries, the clusters have changed in many ways. No one individual has been part of any one of them for very long, though some people have had great influence on the discussion far beyond their time of participation. Most of the clusters have been selective in allowing voices to be heard, sometimes denying participation to people on the basis of their ideas, sometimes on the basis of their gender, race, social or economic class, or sexual orientation. The energy and viability of particular clusters have varied over time, as has the way in which each cluster relates to others. Sometimes they live and work peacefully together; at other times, they fight and kill one another, most often because of loyalties, such as national ones, that override the unity of common faith. The relationships between various Christian clusters and the many non-Christian clusters also change from place to place and time to time: sometimes these relationships are peaceful and sometimes they are violent. As Christians have lived their lives in their clusters—singing, dancing, farming, building, teaching, governing, healing, praying, raising families, giving birth, dying—they have also done theology. Whether as an intense and intentional conversation or as a passing moment in the midst of daily life, Christian people assess their faith and their expressions of faith on a regular basis. Despite all of the changes, the atrocities done in the name of God, and the greater commitment many of the participants have to ideas and practices other than those of their Christian faith, this theological conversation continues today. It has been in process now for two thousand years, and it continues a human conversation about the relationship with the divine that probably dates from our earliest days.

Given that you are reading this book, it is likely that you are in some way part of this Christian conversation. I invite you to participate in a particular form of it, one that is peaceful, inclusive, and intentional—the form I am trying to model in these pages. To say the conversation is *peaceful* is not to deny that some discussions will rightly become heated as we passionately search for the truth; it is to say that physical, emotional, or spiritual violence done in the name of God or in the search for God pollutes the search and dishonors the goal of the conversation. To say the conversation is *inclusive* is not to say that every voice that is heard will, in the end, be seen as offering ideas that are as truthful as every other voice; it is to say that all peaceful voices must be respected and taken seriously. To say the conversation is *intentional* is not to say that the participants will do nothing except explore their world theologically; it is to say that every Christian person makes a part of his or her life the desire for and practice of meaningful theological exploration. For those of you who have not yet been inspired to this level of participation, I hope this book convinces you that lifelong theological exploration is one of the most important tasks you can undertake as a Christian. And I hope you undertake it in the spirit of peaceful and vigorous conversation with the various partners I am about to introduce. For some of you, meeting these partners will be like meeting old friends; for others, it will be more like meeting new ones. For all of us, it should be an invigorating exercise in opening our minds and hearts to a wide variety of important voices.

If we could listen in on all of the Christian clusters when they do theology explicitly, we would find that the ideas being articulated, assessed, and either accepted or rejected emerge from one or more of the following places. While these conversation partners might be differentiated and described in other ways, this way works as well as any I have seen:

1. The Bible
2. Historical approaches to Christian thinking and living
3. The contemporary Christian world
4. Christian religious experiences
5. Non-Christian knowledge and ways of knowing
6. Non-Christian religious traditions

In the characterizations that follow, I provide some definition of each partner and, in order to show you how you might engage it in your own process of self-discovery, give examples of my own engagement with each one. These personal reflections are meant to be illustrations; I do not intend to tell you how to be in conversation with the partners, only to point to possible directions you might take. We begin with the Bible.

The Bible

When I was a pastor in Virginia, I was called in to help facilitate the discussion of a very controversial issue at a local church. My role was simply to help raise the issues the church members would need to consider in making their decisions and to help them find resources within the Christian tradition to inform their discussion. I was attempting to offer various ways of thinking about a particular Scripture passage, based on alternative translations of a biblical verse and the cultural assumptions of a relevant biblical period. Rather suddenly, one man shook his Bible at me and said forcefully, "The King James Version is God's final Word."

I share this example not to take a stand one way or the other on the man's claim, but to remind us of the passion with which we hold onto certain faith convictions. The depths of our convictions and their powerful roles in our lives can make it at least uncomfortable and sometimes frightening to engage in conversation with those who have other convictions—or with ideas in Christian history that are not our own. As Christians, this struggle is especially true when it comes to discussing what the Bible is and what it says. Our fear, though, can hide from us the abundant life we seek to live; overcoming the fear, no matter how difficult, can free us up to deepen and strengthen our convictions and to find a more successful orientation to the world.

Thus, the Bible is the Christian's first conversation partner. To be in conversation with it is to hear its questions and its answers and, ultimately, to be able to give good reasons for one's own faith convictions in light of whatever relevant passages it contains. This is not to say that one's convictions must be grounded in the biblical texts directly or even that they must be consistent with those texts (to say this would imply premature decisions about how to balance the various partners we are going to examine), but that each of us must seriously and honestly engage with these texts that have molded, guided, prodded, confused, inspired, and outraged Christian people and communities for millennia.

What I mean by serious and honest engagement with the Scripture is best shown by illustration rather than definition, so here are two examples. In his book *The Great Reversal: Ethics and the New Testament*, Christian ethicist Allen Verhey reminds us of the claims about Jesus Christ made in 451 CE at the Council of Chalcedon, a gathering of Christian leaders to examine certain theological claims at the center of church discussions.[1] They formulated a way of understanding Jesus Christ that has defined how Christians think of him to the present day: that he is both fully human and fully divine. Verhey suggests that we view the Bible in a parallel fashion: it is both fully God's Word and fully human words. To his mind, this eliminates both the tendency to identify the biblical texts as purely the Word of God, to be obeyed or accepted without question, and the tendency to view the texts as purely human creations that can be accepted or rejected as one desires. His approach is intended to prohibit both attitudes of dismissiveness and attitudes of worship toward what one reads in the Bible. It respects both human epistemological uncertainty, recognizing the human contribution to the texts, and the conviction that God is reaching out to us, affirming that the Bible is not only human but also divine.

You might disagree with Verhey's approach, arguing, perhaps, that he has let too much of the human into Scripture or, alternatively, that he takes God to be too involved in the Bible's words. You might even disagree with him on grounds that some have used for disagreeing with the conclusions of Chalcedon: saying something is both fully one thing and fully another is just incoherent, and theological claims must make sense. Whatever your view, though, you can see that Verhey's is one of the many ways in which we might enter into conversation with the Bible. Verhey is one thinker among countless others in Christian history who have offered a way to approach the Bible in addition to offering views of what it says with respect to particular issues.

Another example of honest and serious engagement with Scripture is the time-honored practice of *lectio divina*, "divine reading." The practice arose out of monastic life in the early centuries of the church and typically has four parts. (You can try it now, if you like; all you need is a Bible and a quiet place to sit and relax.) First, read any passage from the Bible that you choose. Read slowly and with your heart and mind open to whatever meaning may be present for you in the words you are seeing. Be attentive to any word or phrase that may have special importance for you in this particular moment of your life. Second, when you find that word or phrase, pause with it for some time. Let your own sense of what you are hearing guide you in the amount of time you spend, but be as open as you can to hearing what the words and the passage have to say to you. Third, let yourself be guided in prayer around the passage. The type of prayer you use— prayers of intercession for others, wordless prayers in which you simply remain open to anything God may wish to say to you in the moment—does not matter as much as your intention to be open to God's leading in this conversation of the moment. Finally, rest in what you have heard. Sit quietly for a few final moments with the assurance that God loves you and is seeking to guide you in some way.

As with every suggested approach to Scripture, this one requires an examination of assumptions. Should I suppose that God sometimes wants to speak to me personally, as the *lectio divina* practice assumes? Does God seek to communicate with human beings at all? Is God the sort of God who is able to communicate? Is it appropriate to use small passages of the Bible in our theological explorations, or must each book or the entire Bible be taken as a whole? The theologian must ask these kinds of questions as she or he tries to make sense of what the Bible offers to the Christian conversation and how she or he will respond. They can be added to the long list of more general questions asked by scholars and laypeople alike: Is it best to see the Bible as one book or a collection of many books? Should we look to it for specific guidance or simply for a general framework of how to live? Where does it offer historical facts, and where does it offer theological interpretation; what should be our response to either of these? Exactly what is the relationship between the words of the Bible and the Word of God, and what does this mean for us? These and numerous similar questions are always in the background of our conversations with the biblical text, emerging to the forefront from time to time as we probe ever more deeply for what we truly believe.

I remember sitting in the small classroom up on the balcony of St. Andrew's Episcopal Church, in which I grew up, studying the Bible with Mrs. Roberta Anderson. Most of the time, I was her only student, and I was there almost every Sunday. I do not remember anything at all of the content of our discussions, but I certainly remember their tone. I remember holding my Today's English Version of the New Testament as one should hold a sacred text, with reverence and awe. I remember reading and talking about Jesus with her, and I remember her complete trust in the words on the page and God's delivery of them to us, a trust that I have always respected in others even when I have not had it myself. I remember coming away from each forty-five-minute discussion with the clear sense that I had just encountered something essential to my life and to the world's well-being. Approaching Scripture seriously and honestly, which will include academic study as well as approaching its words in faith, should enable you, over time, to clarify your attitude toward it and the role it will play in your life. It should help you to provide significant justification for certain of your faith convictions. It should help you to identify the best convictions possible, not simply justify what you already accept on other grounds. It is the testimony of Christians through the ages that regular engagement with the Scripture, wherever you come down on its role in your life, keeps your convictions centered in the Christian tradition in a way no other single conversation can.

Historical Approaches to Christian Thinking and Living

As important as the Bible is, most of what counts as Christian thought and practice will not be found there. Developed forms of such important doctrines as the Trinity or the Virgin Birth and such central practices as the Lord's Supper were developed in the centuries following the writing of the biblical texts. To attempt to limit your conversation partners to the Bible alone would be to give it an exclusive authority not typically seen in Christian life and practice through the ages, an authority that would discount much that Christians have found to be life-giving.

There are good reasons for exploring the historical dimensions of the Christian conversation, our second conversation partner.[2] First, historical exploration overcomes the frequently unconscious tendency to suppose that everything that comes before us is a mere preface to the true and most important time: our time. But there is no adequate justification for automatically giving current ways of thinking and living priority over chronologically older ones in our theological explorations. Indeed, a bit of historical digging can often provide us with an awareness of valuable knowledge and perspectives that have been lost in the processes of change and passing trends. Second, historical awareness shows us the influence of context on belief and practice: what we think and what we do, including our faith assumptions, are both shaped by a large number of historical factors. Our beliefs and practices are also shaped by present factors that are easier for us to see if we have a grasp on history. This historical consciousness is a crucial dimension of the larger awareness of our epistemological uncertainty. Finally, not to develop a historical consciousness means that we will always try to invent anew what has already been discovered or tested in the past. There is no need to be entrapped by the past (indeed, not being trapped by the past is one major goal of theological and other critical thought), but to be historically unaware of Christian tradition, institutions, thought, and contested boundaries is a bit like having amnesia and only being able to experience today.

Of course, it is impossible to be in conversation with the entire Christian tradition. There are simply too many ideas, practices, people, and clusters of people with whom one would have to engage. Also, many of the voices one might like to hear from the past were never recorded or have been lost and will never be heard. However, to be in conversation with the tradition's broad outlines, and with portions of it in detail, is both possible and necessary. This is especially true because of the apparently random process through which we have encountered various ideas, concepts, and practices in our lives and the intensity with which we hold onto them.

To some extent, we all hold most firmly to what has in some way been passed along to us without examining whether our relatively fulfilled lives might be much better were we to give new shape to our convictions. I may be a devout Episcopalian without knowing anything about Presbyterianism. I may accept one version of the Atonement (how estranged humanity comes to be right with God; more particularly, what it means to say that Jesus Christ died for our sins) without knowing that there are at least two other versions.[3] I may be fully convinced that infants should not be baptized because my church only baptizes more mature Christians. Essentially, the world presents us with some set of historically conditioned convictions, and we accept these without knowing the broader dimensions of the conversation. Ponder this: why is it that we do not accept these terms of ignorance when we are doing more mundane things, such as buying a new car, yet, when it comes to faith, we often remain stubbornly unaware of the enormous collection of alternative Christian beliefs that has come before us? Discerning the convictions on which we base our lives deserves a more intentional and serious approach.

What will you accept into your heart from Christian history? What will you not accept? To what will you remain always open, and about what will you remain never convinced? How do you support your decisions? None of us can give a full response to these questions in a short space, but here are just a couple of personal experiences and reflections as illustrations of what I am asking you to ponder.

It was sometime in high school that I began to do anything like intentional reflection on my deepest faith convictions. I brought into my exploration many years of participation in the Episcopal Church. I carried with me the comfort of its liturgical practice, a sense of the importance of the Bible and the *Book of Common Prayer,* some favorite Scripture passages that seemed to illuminate life, the joy of singing favorite hymns, a regular prayer life based in an understanding of God as watching over me and caring about me, and the sense of community and of being at home that a small, stable church can provide. Although I was attracted to each of these in a particular contemporary manifestation, I also studied many in their historical dimensions.

Conversations and courses in high school started me thinking in new ways about the theology behind this previously unquestioned orientation to life, and my questioning has never stopped. Denominationally, I have listened carefully to Mormon conversations, spurred on originally by an extremely attractive girl named Lilon. She posed new questions to me about the nature of God, the variety of sacred texts, and the preexistence and destiny of human beings, and my answers began to be formed and integrated into my faith convictions. Later, while in graduate school in Chapel Hill, the feel of community, flexible liturgical style, and emphasis on social action in a United Church of Christ church down the road offered me new options for thinking and for worship, an offer I ultimately accepted when I joined the congregation and went on to be ordained in that denomination a decade later. When I attend church these days, I often attend a United Methodist church, whose pastor has something of an evangelical and emotional flair to her, one that attracts me as a counterbalance to my basic theological approach and connects me to a thread in historical Christian worship that I had previously not appreciated. She highlights for me questions about the variety of dimensions of faith and about the involvement of Jesus in our lives, questions that have become part of my ongoing reflections.

Some of my engagement with Christianity's denominational variety has centered on traits central to denominational practice or doctrine, as shaped by their long history, but most of it has focused on conversation with various people who have been important to me. As I converse with what these friends or colleagues bring from their own traditions to the theological table, I am moved to evaluate what I am bringing and to take on new convictions that result in new ways of living. An Orthodox friend's love for icons, the contemplative practices of an Anglican friend, the energy with which a United Church of Christ friend creates worship experiences, the commitment of a friend in the Church of Christ to the Word of God as found in the Bible, the passion for social justice of a United Methodist friend—all of these have led me to encounters with historical dimensions of Christian belief and practice that have made a significant difference in my life.

Beginning to converse with Scripture simply requires opening the Bible and starting to read. Along the way, you will be drawn into deeper discussions about appropriate ways to interpret what you are reading and about the context and meaning of various passages. Beginning to converse with the history of Christian thought and practice is also a matter of just jumping in. It is less important where you start than that you start. There are excellent introductory texts that discuss broad trends in the tradition; there are also excellent collections of readings that focus on particular issues. (You might check the recommended reading list for this chapter as a way of getting started.) Or you could begin with a favorite prayer, hymn, or symbol and ask where it came from and what convictions lie behind it. Wherever you begin, if you are serious and open, you are destined to engage much that can help to shape your convictions and your life.

The Contemporary Christian World

The third crucial conversation partner for giving shape to Christian convictions is what will one day fade into history, namely, Christian life today. Many Christians regularly participate in one or another Christian community, often a church congregation, and may evaluate and test faith commitments in relationship with others in those settings. But Christians are also immersed in a variety of contexts—social, economic, and geographic, among others—that are not obviously based in Christian practices or convictions. Our faith convictions as Christians are discovered, expressed, and tested in our daily lives in the contemporary world, where we face issues that challenge Christian ways of thinking and living as well as issues to which Christian ways can—and should—pose a challenge.

Consider, for instance, the United States' "war on terrorism." As I write, the most public face of this war is in Iraq. Many Christians are fighting there; many national leaders who are Christians are supporting their presence. Prayers for our soldiers and their families can be heard regularly in most Christian churches; occasionally, a prayer for Iraqi soldiers and families will be added. Signs that say "God bless our troops" dot my neighborhood, and I know the war rightly preoccupies the thoughts of many of my neighbors, most of whom are descriptively Christian. Although the resources for thinking about war as a Christian come from far back in Christian history, our faith convictions that are relevant to killing other human beings must always be clarified and tested in the present moment.

Three broad approaches to war appear in Christian history (here we will see clearly the relationship between this partner and the previous one): *pacifism*, which is opposition to war or to participation in war, often based on such biblical teachings as "Thou shall not kill" and "Turn the other cheek" and such biblical imagery as the cross; *just war theory*, which attempts to justify (some argue that it succeeds; others, that it fails) crossing the line from nonviolence to violence by appealing to such conditions as last resort, proportionality, reasonable chance of success, right authority, just cause, and the ultimate intention of peace; and the so-called *holy war* approach, which argues that God sometimes commands war and tends to diminish consideration of limits on the extent of violence that may be used in response to God's command.[4] It is important to understand these approaches and to bring them to bear on our reflections in the current situation, not only because we may contribute meaningfully to creating a better or worse world by the ways we respond or do not respond, but also because which approach we take (and the specific details of that approach) may well say something about how we think God is working in the world. Somewhere in our basic faith convictions, we believe God works one way rather than another in relating to the world. We are likely also to believe something about the implications of this for Christian living. As we bring our faith convictions to bear on the war on terrorism, we may well find them and the world changed in the process. (You might consider, as an additional example, how this process worked in earlier struggles over slavery and civil rights.)

Reflecting on the contexts in which contemporary Christians live brings to mind numerous issues that demand a hearing in our conversation. An incomplete list includes racism, poverty, marriage for gay and lesbian people, the future of the denominational structure of Protestantism, the role of women in the life of the church, the compatibility between Christianity and capitalism, the significance of the disagreement between the Eastern and Western churches on the nature of the Trinity, the role of the pope in guiding the moral lives of Roman Catholics, and the nature of the relationship between allegiance to Christ and allegiance to one's nation. No matter what stance one takes toward any of these issues or the countless others that surround us, exploring the possible stances and defining where one stands requires significant exploration of one's faith if one is going to live well and make it possible for others to do the same.

Another aspect of the contemporary Christian world is the diversity of voices to be found in contemporary Christian theology. Some pieces of writing and some schools of theological thought have a profound influence on the lives of everyday Christians, but others have virtually no impact at all. In part this is because much theological work is not written in a way that is accessible to many who would benefit from engaging it. Sadly, it is often the work that would require serious critical thinking about and assessment of our faith perspectives that is the least accessible. At the same time, there are reflective books on theological issues that are emerging in more popular formats that have a great deal to offer to our search. The reading list for this chapter indicates some of the more accessible and some of the more difficult books that you might find challenging and engaging.

Christian Religious Experiences

The fourth conversation partner in our exploration of faith convictions is the experiences Christian people have that they understand to be religious experiences. Like my experience of peace as I sat on the bench at St. Meinrad's, you may well have experiences of your own that you take to be experiences of God or of the Holy Spirit or simply of something Other that you cannot quite explain. Although it is important to be in conversation with other experiences and not simply one's own, pondering one's own experiences can be a fruitful conversation in itself.

One summer week many years ago, I was in Maryland on a "Spiritual Life of Spiritual Leaders" retreat sponsored by the Shalem Institute for Spiritual Formation. During the week, we had the opportunity to try several different meditative practices, including meditation with an icon. I did not know anything about the sacred history of icons at that time and had certainly never prayed or meditated with one, but decided, in the context of this spiritually refreshing week, to see what the experience was like. For some time, I sat before an icon of Mary and Jesus called Our Lady of Vladimir, focusing on being open to the gaze of God upon me. All of a sudden, I saw myself (in my mind; this was not a vision) in my childhood bedroom, standing beside the bunk beds on which I slept for much of my childhood. I was upset about something. Jesus appeared, calmed me, took me by the hand, and led me out of the front door of the house and up across the front lawn to the road. As the experience faded and my mind came back to the room around me, I became aware of my tears.

This was a powerful experience for me, and a copy of this icon now sits on the table next to my bed at home. My inclination is to say that Jesus healed an inner wound of mine that day, but to be in conversation with religious experiences is neither to dismiss them nor to accept them automatically, but to listen carefully, ponder prayerfully, think critically and decide what they mean and what impact they will have on our thinking and acting. This experience invites me to explore where I need healing, whether there are issues in my childhood that are unresolved, and whether I can accept Jesus' healing and companionship in my life. I must ask whether the experience is best described by saying that a being of some sort (specifically, Jesus) entered my psyche and healed a painful memory, or as a projection of my imagination. I should ponder whether Jesus does, in fact, heal human beings, or Christians, or me. Is this a common occurrence in Christian life or a one-time event for me? What does healing actually amount to in terms of my own well-being? Did something happen here that I was predisposed to understand as I did because of my own background, or is the real activity of the real Jesus the essence of the event? Answering questions such as these can point me in the direction of having a clearer grasp on where I stand in my faith.

As many of you will know, not all religious experiences are pleasant ones. I once had a dream so powerful and awful that I have only been able to describe it as a true encounter with evil. All the details are not important at this point, and dream interpretation is frequently a tricky matter, but the dream included Satan laughing at the violence he was doing against people I cared about. The final scene before I awoke was of me leaning against and sliding down a doorjamb, hugging myself, crying, and repeating "Jesus" over and over again. As with any religious experience, this one raises many theological questions. Is evil personified in this world? Was the dream an encounter with evil that is external to me or evil that is internal to me? Did Jesus in fact save me and, if so, from what? The effect of this dream was to dissuade me for a while from an intensive prayer life I had recently begun, and the entire experience supports a deep faith conviction of mine that there is some sort of cosmic battle between good and evil going on in and around us. Am I right about that? What are the implications for living life well that would flow from such a point of view? Am I and are we better off if we base our lives in such a conviction than if, for instance, we say simply that this was a bad dream and that is the end of the story? These are the kinds of theological issues you must work through in claiming your own theological point of view.

I do not want to give the impression that all of my religious experiences have such dramatic flair to them or that such powerful experiences are the norm for Christians. Neither of these is accurate. The vast majority of religious experiences Christians have are small, often so small as to go unremembered. There is the brief emotional reaction during a sermon, the feeling of camaraderie while working on a service project, the smile or frown at words in the Bible, the sense of compassion for a hurting stranger, the anger at encountering injustice. Such experiences are not, of course, unique to Christians; what makes them fit the category of Christian religious experiences is only that they have been informed or created by the life the one experiencing them has lived in the Christian faith tradition. I have highlighted more intense or dramatic experiences because it is easier to show what I mean when I talk about reflecting on them and because, surprisingly, I find that a significant number of Christians have had such experiences. Not all have had them, however, and you are not somehow less of a Christian if you have not.

For a final example, consider what are sometimes called synchronicities. In a recent e-mail exchange with a friend, she shared with me the experience below.[5] I include it, slightly edited for space, with her permission and simply leave to you the decision about what it means. I should remind you, though, that the answer cannot simply be, "Well, whatever it means to her is fine"; this conclusion dismisses the importance of the conversation and of our conversation partners. Conversations require responses and ongoing engagement.

> I've been having lots of Jungian synchronicities—like finding a yellow swallowtail butterfly with a wounded wing at the left rear wheel of my car. Then two days later finding another one in the same place when the car was in a different location. I've learned that when those things happen it's a sign to pay attention and to try and figure out the symbolism. I finally dug through some literature and found that the butterfly can be a symbol of those creative types who are trying to expand their boundaries, but the woundedness is a warning that you might be doing too much too fast, that others aren't with you. That's kind of funny because I had just announced that I was going to back off some of the more creative parts of my ministry and prove myself in some traditional ways.
>
> Actually, I have been taking seriously my "signs." I think the butterfly warning was strong. It made sense to me and

caught my attention. And so I deliberately tried to make some adjustments in my ministry to be a bit less edgy for a while . . . and that feels okay. And then—you'll love this—having made those adjustments, and thinking as I drove that those were wise decisions, I was buzzed at my windshield by a yellow swallowtail butterfly . . . this one uninjured. It was a bit overwhelming and wonderful.

What experiences have you had that you would call "religious" or "spiritual"? Before proceeding, take a moment to reflect on them. How did you feel? Did they say anything to you about the way God works? What did you learn from them?

Non-Christian Knowledge and Ways of Knowing

Speaking of dramatic stories, here is one that will point us in the direction of pondering the importance of knowledge other than that generated by explicitly Christian contexts. Two pastors I knew who were once involved in a yearlong hospital chaplaincy internship told a story about being on call one night when a woman came into the emergency room complaining of stomach pain and saying she was possessed. The physicians examined her and could not find anything wrong with her, so they called psychiatry to come and take a look. The psychiatrist had no psychiatric solution and joked, "I don't know; maybe she *is* possessed." The chaplains were called. They talked with the woman a bit, and then said to themselves that Jesus' command was to cast out demons in his name. So, there in the middle of the ER, they prayed on and on, more and more loudly, for Jesus to cast out this demon. After thirty minutes or so, the woman vomited and left the hospital feeling fine.

This story reminds us of something important. We do not think it odd that the woman with the stomachache sought medical attention. Nor do we think it odd that the psychiatrists were called in to examine her. Most of us, I suspect, are much more skeptical of the idea that the woman might have been possessed than we would be of the claim that the chaplains simply used language familiar to her to address her problem. What do you think? Was the woman so psychologically attached to her interpretation of her pain that she needed pastoral healing? Had she eaten something that poisoned her, but filtered her experience through a conviction about demon possession? Could she have been right about being possessed? When you have made your decision, ponder why you are more likely to choose demonic possession, on the one hand, or psychiatric or other medical language, on the other, to interpret this provocative experience.

Along with having a variety of ways of viewing the world at our fingertips, we modern people are simply buried in "facts," in countless claims that purport to be true of the world, to correspond to the reality around us and within us. Attached to the onslaught of information is a myth that suggests that we are better off if we know more rather than less. I am increasingly unclear about the strengths and weaknesses of this myth, but there are certainly ways in which I buy into it. I subscribe to three newspapers, one of them online, and probably a dozen magazines, newsletters, and journals. My home and office are filled with books from which I can glean what might as well be an infinite number of facts. I regularly watch at least one news show and sometimes more. In the last couple of days, I have read or heard stories about the war in Iraq, the cloning of a dog in Korea, Bill Frist's position on stem cell research, the world track and field championships, the newest nominee to the Supreme Court, the real estate market, the weather in Florida, Iran's nuclear program, the space shuttle program, and a wide variety of local and regional issues. Each of these stories is somehow incorporated into my overall sense of the world. Does my increased knowledge help me to live a better life? Maybe—or maybe not. We are besieged by facts and surrounded by alternative interpretations of those facts. Some of this knowledge is beneficial to us in seeking to live well, some of it is a distraction from our life plans, and some of it may be harmful to us. It may or may not be helpful that I know how many people were killed in Louisville, Kentucky, last year or how to make a lot of money by "flipping" real estate.

In what ways is all of this knowledge relevant to the development of our Christian faith convictions? How will you decide what interpretations to make a priority in your life? Will you, for instance, take the creationist or evolutionist side when you study biology? Will you look to medicine or to prayer (or to both) when sickness occurs? Will you describe apparent miracles as the work of God or as the working of undiscovered scientific principles? Does God bring death in God's time, or are life and death matters for the natural sciences to explain? Can new discoveries in physics about the nature of the universe tell us anything about God, or are God and physics completely separate orientations to the world? We Christians face these kinds of questions as we enter conversation with nonreligious knowledge. How we respond—and Christian responses run the gamut from overriding all Christian perspectives with knowledge from other places to overriding all other knowledge with Christian perspectives—influences where we stand, what we believe, and how we act; it influences, that is, our deepest assumptions about the world and our role in it.

Non-Christian Religious Traditions

This final conversation partner may be the most controversial one. Christians have not always had a good record when dealing with other faith traditions. True appreciation of and engagement with other ways of seeing and responding to the divine have often been replaced with ignorance, persecution, and violence. Among many Christians, though certainly not all, these approaches are now being replaced with authentic interest. In describing the importance of other faith traditions as conversation partners for Christians, it is worth noting again that to accept a conversation partner is not to accept whatever that partner says. In the same way that one may accept and reject some doctrinal pieces from Christian history, one may choose to accept or reject insights offered by other religious traditions. And one is very likely to give differing weights to insights based on the sources from which they come. As with all of the other partners, what is required is intentional exploration before one can make such decisions.

Christians have typically taken one of three positions when faced with other world religions.[6] Some have held that everyone is called to be a Christian and must respond to that call if they are to find God. In theological studies, this is often called the exclusivist position and appeals, in part, to such biblical evidence as Matthew's Great Commission to support its claim. In Matthew 28:19–20a, Jesus says, "Go therefore and make disciples of all nations, baptizing them in the name of the Father and of the Son and of the Holy Spirit, and teaching them to obey everything that I have commanded you." More directly, in John's Gospel, Jesus says, "No one comes to the Father except through me" (14:6); many Christians use this text as a basis for the exclusivist claim that salvation is in Jesus Christ and only in Jesus Christ. In great contrast, some Christians have taken the pluralist position, which says that God relates to different peoples and traditions in different ways, and that all of these are acceptable to God on their own terms. Many pluralists also note that the use of the word "God" in that statement may in fact not be pluralistic enough, so they replace it with a more general phrase such as "the divine" or "sacred authority." Seeking to find a middle ground, the Christian inclusivist position says that other religions contain some truth but they are not as true or as good as Christianity.

There have been moments in my life when I was close to an inclusivist or, less frequently, an exclusivist position. In the end, though, I am pulled toward the pluralist view for two different reasons. First, it is simply too convenient to take the view that I am one of the fortunate few who are born into the tradition that happens to be the best one. Second, I am generally too aware of the power of my own upbringing to think that the tradition to which I am committed is the tradition to which everyone else should be committed. I remember walking through a museum in Mumbai, India, one day about five years ago, when our tour guide said to me, "You have studied religion, right?" When I said that I had, she continued with, "Can you tell me why the gods only came to India?" She was not especially convinced by my meandering response about pluralism, but her question was a reminder to me that how we are raised has a great deal to do with how we see the world. I am no different in this regard than is she.

Do we need more than such anecdotes to justify calling other faith traditions a conversation partner? The epistemological uncertainty that such experiences reinforce suggests to me that we do not, but there is at least one other significant point to remember. To make other faith traditions a conversation partner is not a new thing for Christians. Christianity has frequently defined itself over against the traditions that surrounded it, whether this was Judaism and paganism in the earliest days, Islam in later days, or New Age and Eastern traditions today. To feel called to define oneself in contrast to other traditions is, in a way, to recognize their importance in the lives of other people. What I am inviting you to do here is to raise this recognition to an intentional and more open level, the level of the true give-and-take of ideas.

Consider just two ideas—detachment and reincarnation—from other traditions as illustrations of the way one's reflections might proceed. I encountered the idea of detachment first in Buddhist thought, I believe, though it is certainly present in Christian writing on meditation. Detachment is simply a way of living in the world without grasping. For Buddhism, desire for things and for permanence is part of what fuels the cycle of death and rebirth from which one ultimately wants to escape; to detach is to cease striving but still live fully. In a society that is so devoted to grasping—possessions, youth, good feelings—detachment is a de-stressing practice and may well free us to live in ways that call to mind a different kind of abundant living than that to which American Christians are so accustomed. My encounter with the Buddhist version of this approach to life actually led me to a deeper engagement with the Christian tradition of meditation and prayer than I would have had otherwise.

What do you think about reincarnation? I have been intrigued with the number of Christians I have met who seriously ponder its possibility. It is not the same, certainly, as the usual Christian view of life after death in which there is a heaven and a hell and, for Roman Catholics, a purgatory. On the other hand, the notion that we are born and reborn until we escape the cycle (are "saved") may complement some Christian views. Personally, I find the notion that we in some way receive multiple chances to find our way through life intriguing from the point of view of pondering the nature of God's love. What it means for each of us to be in conversation with these issues is to continue to ponder them in the light of our developing convictions about the nature and work of God.

Fundamentally, to recognize the limits of our certainty is to be open to exploring insights wherever they may arise. When we understand that we who are Christians are shaped by our contexts and must be uncertain about the reality that may be God, we can also admit that people of other faith traditions may well have discovered things about life that we should know. The only way to find out is not to make judgments prima facie (at first glance, prior to experience) about these other traditions but to enter into honest conversation with them, to the end, as always, of finding ways to live well together.

When All Else Fails, Look for Instructions

Are you feeling overwhelmed? You may well feel as though you have been invited into a swamp! How is one ever supposed to make sense of all the voices that one hears in all the Christian conversations over time? The easy answer, of course, is that one cannot. There are, however, two sets of guidelines that can prove helpful as we try to be sure that we are listening to the best voices we can. Rather like rules of grammar or instructions for putting together a kit of some sort, though far less complete than either of these, these guidelines help us to construct theological points of view out of all the pieces provided by the conversation partners.

Critical Guidelines

In the first chapter, I briefly discussed the problem of suffering, which is often used to argue against traditional understandings of God. As the argument goes, if God is all-powerful, as the Christian tradition typically holds, then he (God is most often a "he" in the tradition) could end all of the suffering in the world. Or, for another spin on this premise, he could have created a world in which there is no suffering. If, as the tradition also says, God is all-good, then God would not want people to suffer. Since the all-powerful God can make his wants come true and since, being all-good, he doesn't want us to suffer, there should be no suffering in the world. Of course, it is obvious to all of us that there is suffering, and so we have argued our way to a contradiction: there is suffering in reality, but there is none by the logic of the matter. In formal terms, this is what is known as a *reductio ad absurdum* argument, one that reduces its premises to absurdity because of the contradiction it generates. Since the world is not a contradictory place in the sense that no statement and its opposite can be simultaneously true (though one of them must be true), one or more of the steps in this argument must be false. There can be no God of the kind typically described by the tradition under the meanings of goodness and power that are typically used. To say it differently, if accepting the traditional understandings of God leads us to a place we cannot logically go, then we must rethink the traditional understandings.

The problem of suffering is the most often used and most powerful of the arguments against traditional Christianity's conceptions of

God. There are ways out of the dilemma it presents, but there is one direction in which we should not be tempted to turn for a solution. I have heard people say things such as, "God is all-powerful and God is all-good no matter what the implications of holding that position may be." This position is very dangerous. It says that critical thinking is irrelevant to theology, so even if my theological views lead to impossible conclusions, I am still going to believe them. This is dangerous because it threatens to make theology, and thus faith, nonsense. If we do not have to adhere to the normal guidelines of critical thinking in doing our theological work, then a Christian could hold any view she or he wanted to hold, whether it made any sense or not. Frankly, there is already enough chaos in the world for people of faith to contribute more in this way. Theological thinking must be critically sound, just as all forms of human critical thought must be.

Consider, now, three questions. First, what is the relationship between the claim that theological discussions must proceed by the rules of critical thinking and the claim that the faith convictions that guide our lives must conform to the same rules? Second, what is the relationship between these claims and the claim that God is logical? Is God not shrouded in mystery for epistemologically uncertain human beings? Finally, is there a specifiable set of critical guidelines to which theological claims must adhere? Even if these questions do not make sense as you read them, I think they will as I discuss their answers.

Typically, rules of critical thinking are applied to statements in an argument. Every argument contains at least one premise (a statement that supports or leads to the conclusion) and a conclusion. The rules enable us to determine whether it is possible to reach our conclusion given our premise(s). This question does not generally arise for single statements such as faith assumptions are likely to be. Yet, at least on the face of it, it does seem reasonable to assume that the guidance provided for our living is going to be more helpful if there are no embedded contradictions in our faith convictions. What would it mean to commit myself to the two assumptions that God wants me to be poor and God wants me to be rich without giving to those two convictions interpretations that make them noncontradictory? At least in general, we would appear to be better off holding that our deepest faith assumptions should be accountable for demonstrating such basic rational requirements as consistency with one another. That response addresses the initial question raised above.

The second question asks whether there is any relationship between the logical structure we are seeking in our faith and theology and the nature of God. Typically, when I suggest the importance of logical reasoning to faith, someone will respond that God's ways are not our ways (see Isa. 55:8) and that God is not subject to the rules of logic. God, it is further claimed, is so far beyond us that we cannot understand God; therefore, we cannot hold God to our standards of rationality. This is then taken to provide the basis for denying that theological and faith claims need to meet those standards, but that is a leap in the argument that is made far too quickly. Remember that a key to the approach of this book is epistemological uncertainty: we simply do not know whether what we think we know about God is actually the case. Therefore, it seems appropriate to hold that we simply cannot know whether God, in nature or in action, abides by what human beings take to be fundamental principles of logic. There is no direct relationship, then, between claiming that our theological and faith claims must adhere to logical principles and claiming that God must so adhere. The latter is unknowable; the former is required by our needs as thinking human beings seeking good lives. We cannot be certain about what God is like, assuming God is truly like anything at all, but in order to live well, we must work to make our faith convictions as logical as possible (without avoiding absolutely the reality of mystery in the cosmos). Otherwise, we risk basing our lives on nonsense.

Finally, is there a specific set of logical principles to which theological claims and faith convictions must adhere? This is an important question, but I cannot answer it. Some of the principles typically used in Western reasoning are *modus ponens*, *modus tollens*, conjunction, noncontradiction, and identity (it will be easier for you to check a dictionary or introductory logic text than for me to try to explain these principles here). However, there are alternative logical systems, including Eastern ones, that are quite different and may or may not have a place in the way we think about God. They might even show us that such virtually unquestioned principles as noncontradiction can be transcended by alternative ways of thinking. This very difficult issue aside, my claim for now is that we should look to basic principles of Western critical thought for help in making our Christian theological arguments and clarifying our Christian faith convictions, even as we remain open to changes in our list of guidelines.

Ethical Guidelines

One implication of the above sections on critical guidelines is that our theological claims and faith convictions must be subject to critical assessment *even if God is not*. Similarly, our theological claims and faith convictions are subject to *ethical* assessment even if God is not. We cannot know to what extent God adheres to Western (or any other human) moral principles, but theology and faith as human endeavors must be guided by the best moral insights we can identify.

Since almost any example I use to make this point is going to be controversial, I might as well present one that is likely to raise eyebrows among many readers. Personally, I cannot accept the notion that God sentences those of us who do not believe in certain things to eternal punishment in the flames of hell. As a modern Christian, you may well have reconsidered claims such as this one as much as I have, by turning eternal suffering into eternal separation from God or something else that sounds, on the face of it, less agonizing. But I cannot buy, either, the notion that God allows particular choices we might make in this life to have eternally negative consequences (and perhaps not even eternally positive consequences, but that is another story). I am not denying that actions have consequences. I am not even denying, at least at this moment, that God rewards and punishes. What I am denying is that a God who loves us and who is so mysterious to us would be acting morally in either sentencing us to eternal agony or allowing our actions to separate us from God for eternity.

I have to confess that, as I wrote the paragraphs above, I quivered just a bit. Some notion from my past that suggests that those who deny hell might just end up there is enough to make me a bit queasy about offering the bold statements I have made. But the notion that we could be making eternally significant choices under conditions of uncertainty, at least where significance concerns the possibility of us reaching some kind of final happiness in God's presence (what is often called heaven), strikes me as suggesting that God is not even as good as the best human standards of morality. My human father, with his imperfect and human love, would never sentence me to eternal punishment; there is no crime great enough that would prompt that response from him. To suggest that God, whose love is traditionally held to be far greater than ours, would sentence me to such a thing seems outrageous.

I may or may not be correct in my view about hell here, but the most important issue is whether I am successfully illustrating for you the relevance of moral principles to faith convictions. I am saying that faith convictions such as the view that God will send me to eternal punishment if I do not believe in Jesus should be eliminated as potential guiding convictions for our lives because of their dependence upon a view of God as immoral. We can, of course, debate exactly which principles or ideals or virtues have this function in our theological work, but that fact only reiterates the conditions of uncertainty under which we are working.

It might seem as though this discussion is unnecessary because so many of what we take to be important ethical principles are to be found in the conversation partners. In examining Scripture, we find such commands as "love your neighbor." In pondering current Christian life, we have to consider how God wants us to think about hunger. Nonreligious discussions offer competing theories on the good life and on right and wrong. Buddhism, one of the major world religions, holds up the ideal of the Bodhisattva[7] who makes a huge personal sacrifice in order to point all of us to salvation. Given this, instead of talking about these guidelines apart from our conversations with the partners, we could simply say that these moral elements of the conversation partners are relevant to us in our considerations along the way.

I have chosen to give ethical guidelines, like critical guidelines, a more prominent role for two reasons. The first is autobiographical and has to do with a lifelong concern to know and do what is right (though I have not, of course, always reached my goal). The second is that, as we have seen, in a world of uncertainty our faith convictions must be assessed in large part by their ability to enable us to live well. Given the major role of the moral dimension in any view of what it means to live well, it makes sense that ethics will play a large part in evaluating faith convictions. As theological arguments and claims express faith convictions, they will be similarly evaluated. Our faith convictions should express the highest human conceptions of morality and ethics. Whatever God may be about, we have no right to act immorally or to hold as guiding convictions views that are unethical or that breed immoral lives.

To make this second point in a bolder way: ethics is the guarantor against crazy theology. If someone shoots an abortion doctor and claims to be following God's command, we must declare them immoral (or psychologically unbalanced), not say that they are answering to a higher authority. I once heard a well-known rabbi say, referring to the famous story of Abraham and Isaac, "If you think God is telling you to sacrifice your only son on a mountain, you're wrong. Seek psychological care." This would be my position as well. The key here, again, is uncertainty. *We simply cannot be certain enough of God's words to us, if indeed God speaks any words to us, to act contrary to humanity's highest and most rationally defensible moral standards on grounds of hearing God's voice.* Just as faith convictions and theological positions need to be logically defensible, so they need to be morally defensible.

One of the questions I asked in my discussion of logical principles was whether there are specific principles that apply to theology and faith. A similar question should be raised here. Are there specific moral principles, theories, virtues, or ideals that should guide our faith convictions and theological claims? My answer has to be as vague here as it was with respect to logic. It would be difficult not to accept as normative for Christians a principle against harming others or in favor of the fair distribution of resources, as well as the virtues of fidelity and courage. Yet, in the end, the only claim I can make with confidence here is that we should look to the highest moral appeals of human reflection in evaluating our theological arguments and faith convictions.

A Final Word

Perhaps the central issue that will differentiate us as we ponder all of these things is how we should weigh or balance particular ideas or conversation partners. Some of us will argue for the supreme importance of Scripture, while others will lift up a moral principle such as love of neighbor and measure all else by it. Some Christians will accept parts of historical Christianity as a conversation partner, but adamantly reject other parts; other Christians will head in the exact opposite direction. Some will accept evolution as an appropriate theory for understanding human development; others will insist on affirming the biblical story of creation in a way that rejects that theory. This is the way of Christian history and human thought in general, and it will continue to be so. There is, however, more that we can say about the effort to balance the partners and their voices.

The convictions I am encouraging each of you to articulate, assess, and either choose or dismiss are declared in the human heart. In this sense theology is inescapably autobiographical. What I declare theologically, what I affirm faithfully, are things that have taken shape in my own heart, intentionally or unintentionally, and that enable me to live my life, and, ultimately, all of us to live our lives, with reasonable success. The theological process is the process of examining these things in order to raise the reasonably successful life to life abundant, but the entire process depends upon my heart, the core of me where my deepest convictions reside. In all that I am writing here, I am trying to point us toward the depths of our hearts, toward those inner convictions on which we rely to make our lives comprehensible and worthwhile. The informed heart is not a conversation partner, but the final arbiter of what we must accept to live well. It is the resting place of our convictions about those things that matter most, the things of God, even while we continue to explore these things and to give them new shape. In some sense, then, taking all the partners and arguments into account, the human heart, communally shaped and expressed, is the place where the partners are balanced.

Questions for Reflection

1. What is your first impression of my list of Christian conversation partners? Are there any with which you can imagine yourself having a difficult time conversing? If so, why? If not, why not?
2. What is your view of the Bible? Define your terms carefully. Where did this view come from, and why do you hold it today?
3. What would you say if you had to give a ten-minute review of Christian history?
4. Have you read anything you would consider to be contemporary theology? What did you learn from it that you can make a part of your current conversations?
5. Think of a Christian religious experience that you have had. If you think God or Christ or the Holy Spirit were involved, how so? What makes you think the experience was something other than a normal human one? Did you learn anything about yourself or about God from the experience?
6. How and in what ways should Christians care about such non-religious forms of human knowledge as science?

7. Do you consider yourself to be an exclusivist, an inclusivist, or a pluralist when it comes to encountering other faith traditions? Why do you take the position you do? What are the arguments for other points of view, and why do you reject them?

8. Is God logical? Should we be? Is God moral? Should we be?

9. In trying to reach your own theological viewpoints, how do you believe these conversation partners should be balanced as authorities? How would you argue in support of your position?

4

Exploring Theological Issues:
Basic Steps

M any years ago, a counselor pointed out to me that
there are times when some emotional issue will
simply bubble up to the surface of our conscious-
ness, either gently or dramatically, and that these are opportunities
for us to grow in self-understanding. I have found that paying attention to such moments makes a significant positive difference in my
life. I have also found that it is not only emotional issues that can rise
to the surface of our consciousness, but that faith convictions may also
demand our attention. We lie awake at night wondering whether anyone was really listening to the prayers we just said. We wonder why
our friend or family member had to die and where she might be now.
We think there is a heaven and one day find ourselves explaining to a
roommate how to get there. We begin to fear that we are going to hell
for something we have done. We stand in the voting booth wondering whether God cares which way we vote. We meet the world's greatest guy and figure it must have been part of God's plan for us. We sing
the words "God bless America" and find it difficult to believe that
God has singled out America for special attention. Sometimes and
unpredictably, life just seems to present us with these opportunities
to understand the faith dimensions of our lives more fully and to live
more richly.

The second half of this book is going to focus on the issue of voca-tion—what does God want me to do?—an issue that I see bubbling up within so many of the students, friends, and colleagues with whom I speak on a regular basis. However, since the general steps for inves-tigating any theological issue are the same, reading the remainder of this book will also provide you with an opportunity to wrestle with any theological issue that might be demanding attention in your walk with God. So, before moving on to discuss vocation, I explain, in this chap-ter, the steps for the theological examination of any issue. If your issue is something other than vocation, or if you want to ponder questions in addition to the vocation questions, you will find here the tools you need to progress in self-understanding and in deepening your faith commitments on any issue at all.

I invite you, therefore, to take a few minutes and name the faith or theological issue that is most pressing for you right now. By the way, I know what you are thinking. If you are like me, you are going to ignore this invitation. Were I to read the first sentence of this para-graph in someone else's book, I would typically dismiss it either because I felt confident that all my life issues were resolved (a com-mon illusion) or because I just wanted to get through the book and did not want to have to put in the effort to think concretely about my life. I would figure that I would see what the approach was all about and then come back to it sometime, if I felt like it. Of course, I would never feel like it. I would simply move on to the next book and read about another approach and never actually ponder my own life. If you are not tempted to skip the invitation, then I admire your determi-nation to think carefully about your faith. If you are so tempted, then I urge you not to give in. My own experience is that these issues are never easy to ponder but that the work is virtually always worth the effort. So, if you have wondered why it could possibly be important to hold that God knows everything (a quality known as omniscience) or that God is all-powerful (omnipotence); if you have wanted to believe that Mary appeared at Fatima and Medjugorje but cannot quite accept the stories; if you are fearful of hell and hopeful of heaven; if you see similarities in the birth stories of Jesus and the Bud-dha and wonder how that can be; if you are filled with despair and cannot seem to find any meaning in life; if you are convinced that sex before marriage is unacceptable to God but have friends who tell you otherwise; if you think the idea of saying marriage vows publicly amounts to nothing more than performing for a piece of paper; if you think the Trinity must make sense but have no idea what sense it makes; if some passages in the Bible drive you crazy even though you want to believe them, then I sincerely hope you accept this invitation to do some serious theological work.

❖❖❖❖❖❖❖

The theological process that leads to being able to claim a personal faith conviction on a given issue is fairly straightforward.

1. *Identify your issue.* This seems easy enough, but it is not always a simple process to state our concerns clearly and carefully. The more precisely you can state your concern, however, the easier it will be to explore it without wandering in unhelpful directions.

2. *Say why you care about this issue.* What is it about your life that inspires you to reflect on this issue at this time? What does caring about this issue imply for your life? What outcome do you hope for that makes pondering this issue worthwhile to you? This step helps you to engage your issue as deeply as possible by highlighting for you its autobiographical importance.

3. *Articulate your current faith convictions about your issue.* You need to start wherever you are. This might begin by stating your gut response to the issue, but the more critically you can assess your view, the higher will be the quality of the raw material you will have to work with later.

4. *Take your current stance and enter into conversation about it with the partners identified in chapter 3.* You might think of this as testing your hypothesis. From this fourth step, you will emerge with a new understanding (or a confirmation of your old one) and be ready to make a new commitment. Although your faith journey may well cycle back through the same questions another time, for the moment you will have identified a place you can stand with awareness and fully chosen conviction.

5. Finally, *you must discover what kind of world is created when you live out your new commitments.* This real-life test is the final one and can take years, but it will ultimately let you know whether your conviction is worth keeping or should be replaced.

Step One: Stating the Issue

It may be very easy for you to identify your issue and to put it into words. One of the issues I named above may be one you have been trying to figure out for a long time. It may be that something has occurred in your life recently that weighs on your faith. It may be that simply being asked to state your issue triggers a response from you that you cannot explain but that makes clear to you what you should be exploring theologically. Or it may be that it takes a couple of days of paying attention to your life and listening to your heart before an issue emerges into your awareness.

Perhaps no issue appears quickly for you. In this case, you might try one or both of the following two exercises. The first exercise is to ask yourself what was the last faith conviction or theological claim you heard someone express that caused you to have a significant emotional response. Did you become annoyed when someone urged you to examine your faith? Did you become angry when you heard a preacher claim that all non-Christians are going to hell? Did you rejoice when a friend shared that his prayer request had been answered? Did you celebrate when you finally stopped receiving invitations to a Bible study? Were you elated when the person you are dating agreed to attend church with you? Often, the issues that inspire the greatest emotional response in us are the ones especially worth examining further. Our heightened emotions suggest that our convictions in the identified area are deeply important to us. Since such deep convictions influence our lives in a myriad of ways, assessing and reassessing them is virtually always appropriate.

A second exercise that can help you to identify issues that are of pressing theological importance to you is to try to identify your level of commitment to various faith convictions or theological claims. On a piece of paper, draw a line with "high commitment" at one end and "low commitment" at the other. Take fifteen minutes and name as many faith convictions or theological issues as you can, placing them on the line in a way that illustrates your level of commitment to them. If you are deeply committed to the view that there is a God, for instance, indicate this at the "high commitment" end of the continuum. If you are fairly committed to the idea that God is all-powerful, but not as committed as you are to the idea that God exists, note "God is all-powerful" in the appropriate place. If you are about as uncommitted as one can possibly be to the notion that there is a heaven or that its streets are paved with gold, represent your commitment level to that claim accordingly. After fifteen minutes, stop and look at your continuum. You might choose to focus your theological attention on any one of the issues you have named, since they have come to mind so quickly, but I suggest picking one of those that is near one of the ends. Understanding as fully as possible either something to which we are greatly committed or something to which we are minimally committed can be equally helpful as we try to identify who we are and how we need to live our lives.

Once you identify your issue, try to state it carefully, perhaps by putting it in the form of a question. This approach can deepen your personal engagement with the issue and help you approach it as something you truly want to know. The issue is not salvation, but "Am I saved?" or "Are others saved?" The issue is not omnipotence, but "Is God all-powerful?" Or, even more personally, "Can God heal me?" The issue is not vocation, but "Is God calling me?" "Should I get married?" "What career should I choose?" You will have plenty of chances along the way to refine your question, but get as close as you can now, before moving to the next step.

Step Two: Understanding Why You Care

I was talking with someone recently about her theological journey, and she was standing firm to her claim that God is all-powerful. I was not arguing with her view, but I was trying to help her clarify the issues. I asked her why she cared whether or not God is all-powerful. Did the answer make any difference for her faith or her life? Her response was that her life was out of control and she needed to know that "someone out there" was in control of it. As you can imagine, this was an important recognition that enabled us to have a conversation focused on some of the deeper issues about her life and her relationship with God.

If I could make only one recommendation about this step, it would be that you neither ignore nor be satisfied with the obvious. Avoid both temptations. Sometimes we care for clear and straightforward reasons but spend a lot of time thinking there must be something else to it: it couldn't be *that* simple, could it? At other times, we name a couple of superficial reasons but do not want to seek the deeper and more important ones. Giving in to either of these temptations will work against you in your exploration, so it is worth pausing and relaxing with this step until you are sure you understand clearly yourself and your relationship to the issue.

Step Three: Developing a Hypothesis

Another key to successful personal theological exploration is to begin exactly where you are. This is why I have asked you to pay attention to what issue is emerging into your awareness today, to ponder why your issue is of personal significance for you, and to reflect on all of these things within the context of an autobiographical understanding. You cannot make any personal faith progress by disengaging yourself from the issue at hand.

Whatever your issue or question may be, you likely already have some response to it. Often this will be a quick gut reaction based on what you hope the answer is or on what you were taught growing up, or perhaps you have worked on the issue before so that your response is based on some serious investigation and you want to continue that work now. Somehow or other, though, you have probably formulated a tentative answer; this is the time to articulate it and do an initial critical examination of it. The result of this will be the raw material that you will then take to the conversation partners, whether for the first time in your life or the tenth. Your conversations will lead you more deeply into the question, into possible answers, and into your own personal conviction.

You may be asking, "How do I get from my initial gut response to the raw material that you are talking about?" My suggestion is to focus on three things: meanings, assumptions, and implications. What do the words that you are using mean? What are the assumptions you must examine to help you to clarify your point of view? What are the implications of your view for living and promoting a good life? Here are a few randomly chosen faith convictions you might be examining and some examples of critical questions that could facilitate the next statement of your view, the statement that will act as your raw material.

Sample Conviction 1: Salvation is through Jesus alone.

1. What is salvation?
2. From what do we need to be saved, and what does it look like when we are?

3. What is the meaning of "through" in this case? How is salvation "through" Jesus?
4. Were I deeply committed to this, how would I live? Is this an acceptable life?
5. Does holding this conviction contribute to global flourishing? How or how not?
6. What makes Jesus so special?

Sample Conviction 2: The quality and quantity of suffering in the world proves that there is no God in the traditional Christian sense.

1. What, exactly, is suffering?
2. Why does suffering raise questions about God? What is it about the traditional view of God that makes suffering a problem?
3. What understanding of God might alter our understanding of suffering?
4. Are there any reasons for holding onto traditional conceptions of God?
5. Can the existence or nature of God be "proven"? Is proof a theological concern?
6. Why do the quality and quantity of suffering have anything to do with this argument?
7. Is there a theological difference between one person in despair and a thousand people starving?

Sample Conviction 3: God is on the side of the poor.

1. What, exactly, does "on the side of" mean here?
2. Is "poor" an economic category—or something else?
3. What are the implications of being on the side God is not on? Does being on God's side (or having God on your side) matter?
4. How should we treat people who are poor and people who are not poor if God is on one side?
5. Where do we draw the line between those who are poor and those who are not poor?
6. On what issues does God take sides?

These sample convictions are not intended to be issues for which you go searching for new answers. Any one of them might be an issue on its own. For now, the goal is to clarify what you are already thinking, not to begin the search for new answers. If you take your gut response and then carefully and critically think about what you mean and what you do not mean, whether or not you have to revise something in your statement because you have noticed the presuppositions on which you are relying, and whether you honestly think that your point of view contributes to the good life for all of us, you will have either affirmed your initial response or transformed it into one that articulates well your current conviction. This is the hypothesis you will take to the conversation partners.

Step Four: Conversations

By engaging in conversations with your partners, you can test your conviction as a hypothesis as you try to clarify it and live the best life possible. Learning from the ways the partners challenge or affirm your conviction will let you know whether it is an appropriate one for you to hold and a legitimate one on which to base your life. You will discover whether you can continue to be committed as you are or whether there are good reasons for you to reconstruct your theological point of view.

You should not miss the impact of what you are about to do. Put starkly, the question at hand is whether you can, from this moment on, legitimately believe what you now believe. Can you remain committed to or continue to base your life on your current faith conviction? If the answer is yes, then you will need to be sure your actions are witnessing to your convictions; if the answer is no, then you need to envision anew at least one of the convictions on which your life may have been resting. Theological legitimacy is of vast importance, so you should not enter this exploration lightly. Taken seriously, it can change your life.

Given the importance of this process, I am going to digress briefly here and consider one frequent reaction, and one important objection, to what I am encouraging you to do.

Examining Life

A frequent reaction to the idea that theological exploration might change one's life goes something like this: "I am going to believe what

I want to believe and live the way I want to live, and that's all there is to say about that. You cannot make me change my faith." Well, you are right. You *are* going to believe what you want to believe (unless your beliefs are so at odds with reality that you are virtually forced to change them), and you *are* going to live the way you want to live (that is, unless you want to live in a way that is simply impossible for who you are or is so at odds with the rest of society that you are forcibly stopped). I am not talking, however, about what you or I *will* do; I am talking about what we *should* do. We should commit our hearts and minds to theological claims that we can justify, and free ourselves from those claims that we cannot justify.

Two important questions arise at this point. First, why is justification so important? Why would it be wrong for me to commit myself to whatever I want to commit myself to and, therefore, to live in whatever way I want to live? Exactly what sort of "wrong" is this? Second, is it really possible to justify one theological claim over another? Can we really even do what I am claiming we need to do?

As I said in an earlier chapter, the human condition is one of seeking to make sense of the world and to live well in the midst of uncertainty, of being forced to choose as part of being human, and of being invited in each moment to define ourselves and our world in response to a universe that continually poses questions. If you acknowledge that this is our state of being, then it should follow that one of your goals will be to center your life on claims for which you can give good and convincing reasons (which is what justification is all about). If you do not accept this view of the human condition, then I invite you to consider the possible problems—practical and moral ones, especially—with the point of view you are advocating. If you still do not buy the claim, then I would revert to my suggestion in chapter 3 that giving shape to theological claims in conversation with these partners is simply what Christians do. I would also argue that no Christian can, as a matter of logical, ethical, and theological consistency, live outside of a certain broad framework and remain meaningfully Christian. This may not require you to ponder what you believe, but it does eliminate many ways of life you might choose.

Is it really possible to justify one faith conviction over another? Can taking my tentative conviction or hypothesis into a conversation with the named partners actually identify for me whether it is more justified to base my life on one conviction over another? What is the relationship between the conversation we are about to undertake and betting my life on one faith stand rather than another?

Since this is a crucial element in theological reflection, ponder what I am about to say as fully as possible before actually engaging the partners. *The best we can do in life is to think and live as we have good reasons to think and live.* The insight that "the unexamined life is not worth living" and its corollary, that it is worth living the examined life, are wisdom from the ages, not mine alone. Humanity's great gift is to be able to assess who we are and what we are doing and, through our assessment and our choice, transform ourselves into what we would rather be or what we must be if we are to live well. Part of what you have been doing as you have worked through this book, I hope, is to take notice of some of the ways and places where you have not simply accepted whatever you were told but have done your best to live your own life well. Serious engagement with these conversation partners will continue your quest. It will show you on what you have good reasons to bet your life and on what you do not. It will not guarantee that you have found the ultimate truth, for we human beings do not have access to that, but it will give you the most convincing argument possible within the Christian framework that is your home. I suggest that you ponder this until you can commit yourself to the process ahead; otherwise, you are likely to let the very human fear of change about matters of faith rule you instead of letting God guide your way.

Some will voice an objection much like this one from a good friend and strong Christian: "I just don't feel well enough grounded in our latest reflections to be willing to subscribe to them and violate the underlying tenets of Christianity." This book is not intended to encourage violating any tenets of Christianity. I am not out to destroy anyone's faith, Christian or otherwise. However, most of us are so uncritical with our faith that we are not even clear what we mean when we say we believe something, and, furthermore, being so uncritical means that many of our faith convictions are simply handed to us by others with no intention on our part to claim them or reject them. This is appropriate for the earliest parts of our life, but maturity requires the work, and play, of serious examination and choosing for ourselves.

Now, what if by doing this critical theological work we end up altering, rejecting, or "violating" the tenets of Christianity? First, the basic tenets of the Christian faith have been interpreted in numerous different ways throughout history, and many of these interpretations have weathered theological crises of all kinds; the continued examination of them is entirely appropriate to the history of faith, and there is a great deal of room within the faith for different interpretations. Second, I would argue that *if the tenets of our faith are not true in the sense of enabling us to live the best possible lives together with the rest of creation, then they should be rejected.* Finally, if you are a Christian, then you do not exist over against Christianity and its tenets. You are part of the ongoing shape of the faith, which includes the continuing critical assessment of all that Christians have stood for in the past and stand for today. The shape of Christianity for tomorrow— whether it contributes to life or to death, for instance—is in the hands of today's Christian faithful.

Too Many Clusters!

You may wish to continue pondering the previous paragraphs for a while, but if you are ready to move on, then we must immediately face a challenge that arises when we begin to converse with our partners. There are too many clusters of people and strands of conversation through history, even Christian history, for us to master all the parts of the conversation; indeed, we never even hear of many of the clusters or their conversations. The exploration in which we are taking part has been taking place for thousands of years with billions of people. Indeed, even if my only conversation partner were the Bible, it would be impossible in my lifetime to find anything like a final answer to the question of whether I can give good reasons to accept any meaningful theological hypothesis. Among other challenges, I would have to settle a number of difficult problems of interpretation raised by biblical scholars through the ages before knowing what I might be able to conclude from the stories. This problem is not restricted to theological work, and virtually everyone in every academic field is simply doing the best he or she can to participate in a conversation that is beyond the possibility of intellectual mastery. However, this fact need not distract us, for we are not seeking the final answer (to which we do not have access), but merely sufficiently good reasons to go one way rather than another in claiming our faith stance.

What is your level of familiarity with the Bible? The history of Christian thought and life? Other faith traditions? The other partners? Theological reflection on each of these? Your response to these questions will determine how you proceed. If you are very familiar with all of these, then you are prepared to proceed with the conversations ahead. Simply locate bits of the conversation that affirm your conviction and bits that challenge it, balancing these out according to the guidelines of critical thought, ethical reflection, and your own life and heart.

If, however, you are less familiar with the partners and the many approaches to reflection upon them, here are some suggestions for how to proceed. Each of these suggestions might be discussed and debated almost endlessly, but I am going to give them to you as a kind of "top-nine list," though in no particular order of importance, for moving from your hypothesis into conversation with the partners.

1. Pray, study, and serve others.
2. Ask about what you don't know; seek multiple answers and weigh them.
3. Test all possible answers critically and ethically. Be sure to listen openly to points of view that are not similar to your own.
4. Engage the Bible and let it engage you. Learn to use a concordance and commentaries. Perhaps the best single-volume commentary is *The New Jerome Biblical Commentary*, edited by Raymond E. Brown, Joseph Fitzmyer, and Roland Murphy (Englewood Cliffs, N.J.: Prentice Hall, 1990).
5. Read Huston Smith's *The Illustrated World's Religions: A Guide to Our Wisdom Traditions* (San Francisco: HarperSanFrancisco, 1994), along with other helpful books. The reading lists offer some recommendations.
6. Find a spiritual mentor.
7. Be part of an honest, open, and exploring community, of two people or ten. Chapter 7 discusses this step in more detail.
8. Do not uncritically privilege one of the conversation partners over the others. Each one makes its own contribution to the process.
9. Become like a little child (see Matt. 18:3); trust in God. Become like an adult; think for yourself. Balance these two.

Step Five: What Kind of World?

I wrote in chapter 2 that "Christian faith is reliance upon a set of articulable but frequently unarticulated and unconscious assumptions or convictions that, taken together, demonstrate the centrality of Jesus to a person's relationship with God and provide her or him with resources to live well in an uncertain world." Our convictions about the world and how we should live in it must be tested, finally, by their implications for creation: the environment, human life, and other life, everything that our convictions impact. The final test of our faith, the final theological test, is what kind of world our convictions support or create. Additional reflections on this will wait for the final chapter.

You now have the theological tools you need to stand where you must stand on matters of faith. Frankly, it is good for you, for me, and for the world that we apply these tools and more deeply understand who we are and who we will be. You can cycle through these steps as many times and on as many different issues as you like. If you want to do more of this important preparatory work, simply head back to the appropriate place in this chapter and work through it again. For an extended illustration of the process applied to a significant theological question—does God call us and, if so, to what?—head to the next chapter, where we begin to explore together whether God is calling you and what God is calling you to do.

Questions for Reflection

1. Are any theological issues bubbling up for you at this moment in your life?
2. Assuming you have stated your issue, what were the competitors for your immediate attention? Why is the one you chose the most important one?
3. Do you know other people who have very different gut reactions than you to your particular issue? How do you explain that?
4. Would you support or reject my claim that the best we can do in life is to think and live as we have good reasons to think and live? How would you support or reject this claim? What are the arguments on your side of the debate? On the other side?

5. How would you assess my "top-nine" list? Are there parts of it you think would help you and parts of it you think are irrelevant to your life?
6. What does it mean to test faith convictions in the real world? Does it make sense to do this? Have you done it before? What happened?

5

Vocation, Part 1:
Developing a Hypothesis

Viewed from the perspective of this moment, everything in your life is a given. This is simply a truth
about us and something with which we must deal.
Our genetic makeup, our environment, and our choices have all
played a part in getting us here, but today we are where we are. In
my case, I teach theology at a liberal arts college; I have a sister who
lives in Florida; my car has a scratch on the passenger's side; I have a
house I like and two cats who live in it with me; my beard is graying;
I am an American; I have no children. Each one of us can make our
own similar list. Whatever the influences and decisions that have
brought us to where we are, we are here and, in this moment, are
essentially handed all of these things with which we must deal. We
can have any number of feelings about what we have been handed,
but that will not change the fact that we are who we are and must live
our life on that basis.

Christian conversations about vocation recognize this "givenness"
of our condition and express a conviction that, in some way and to
some extent, God is the giver. For example, it may be that God, working through my parents, gave me a sister because of some eternally
significant lessons God wanted to teach us all about the meaning of
family. On the other hand, now that I have a sister, God may give me

certain responsibilities I would not otherwise have, but God may have had no hand in creating our family with this particular configuration of people. These describe different perspectives on the fact that I have a sister, but both highlight the role of God as the one behind certain facts of my life. Christian conversations about vocation typically accentuate both the condition of being a Christian, on the one hand, and various social roles and sets of responsibilities, on the other, singling them out as "callings," ways of life that God wants you or me in particular to live. God's "activity" in calling us is not necessarily different than God's activity in other situations where God reveals to us certain ways to live (consider the giving of the Ten Commandments, for instance), but the roles themselves are ones Christians throughout history have highlighted.

God's calls to us are held to be discernable. Over time, human beings have continually recounted a wide variety of experiences of feeling "at home" in one place rather than another, of sensing that one way of life "fits" better than another, of being pulled or led or dragged by an event or series of events toward some action or role, of understanding ourselves as being in sync with the universe when living in one way and not when living in another, of feeling in harmony with the world instead of in disharmony, or of having a deep and abiding joy about our life or some part of it that continues regardless of changing circumstances. These are frequently seen as indicators of what God wants us to be doing and of what God does not want us to be doing. The positive experiences, when they remain over a significant period of time, even if occasionally disappearing because of difficulties we face, are taken to be signs of God's call; the opposite experiences, especially when they create a negative balance over time, are taken to be signs that we are on the wrong path or in the wrong place.

We are about to explore this idea that God calls us to live in some ways rather than others. We will try to discover the answers to such puzzles as whether God is calling you to pursue a particular career, to be married or single, to be a mother or a father, to serve the church as a pastor or teacher, or, once you are in any of these places, to live your role in a particular way. We will examine the notion that there are certain signals or indicators that we are on the right path, doing what we are "meant" to do, and see how precisely we can describe these. We do all of this in the context of the approach to thinking theologically that you learned in the previous chapters.

Were a pollster to approach me on the street and ask me whether I believe that God calls us to live in certain ways rather than others, I would say yes. Were the question whether I think God has called me to my current work, I would say yes. If the question were whether God calls many different people to many different things, I would say yes. In each case, however, I would not be saying much more than the high percentage of Americans who tell pollsters that they believe in God. In order for this affirmation to begin to be meaningful, we would need to ask follow-up questions such as: In which God do you believe? What is your God like? What does your God do? What do you mean by "believe"? How do you orient your life differently because of your belief? No one would discover much about me or the way I locate myself in the world by hearing that I believe, or even that I am firmly convinced, that God calls me or us to something or to some place. Theologically meaningful conversation depends upon our willingness to be as clear and precise as we possibly can about what we mean when we share our faith and name our convictions. Even more, faith convictions require precision, for the most important reason of all: we are basing our lives on them. The first step we need to take, then, is to state the issue carefully.

Step One: Stating the Issue

With any abstract idea—consider democracy or love, for instance—there are a large number of issues that might really be at the heart of one's concern but which disappear when we think we all know what we are talking about. In the case of vocation (remembering the importance of stating our issues in the form of questions), the following are among those that might be our central concern: Is there a particular career path that God wants me to follow? Are there ways that God wants me to live and ways that God wants me not to live? Does God have a plan for me? If so, what is it? What can we learn about ourselves given that we have the idea that God calls to us? Does God call everyone or only certain people? Does God call everyone to something different? How can I discover what God wants me to do, assuming God wants me to do something in particular? Do I have to be a Christian to be called by God? Does God call everyone to be a Christian? If I say no to God's call, what will happen? Would God call me to something I really do not want to do? You can quickly see that saying we are going to explore vocation does not get us very far—or it threatens to immerse us in a virtual swamp of questions and issues. We are not able to avoid all the complexities that any serious theological work brings with it, of course, but we do want to narrow our focus if at all possible.

My first shot at identifying the question I really wanted to ask was to type, simply, "Does God call?" After writing this question, I stared out the window for several minutes and then took an early lunch. It was almost two days before I returned to the computer. Frankly, many theological questions emerge from such depths of the human soul, attempt to reach into such mysterious places in the cosmos, and demand answers that are so inexpressibly important to the ways in which we live, that sometimes all I can do, and perhaps all any of us *should* do, is to sit in awe. Eventually, in order not to be paralyzed by a recurring awe response, however, we should remind ourselves that both the question of whether God calls and the question of whether God calls you and me in particular are a bit different than what we are really able to answer.

Earlier, I characterized Christian theology as "the disciplined approach to the interpretation and assessment of Christian faith convictions that invites us into the depths of ourselves to discover and claim where we must stand in order to make sense of our lives as we seek to live well." Assuming this understanding of the work we are doing, the appropriate theological question is not whether God calls, a question the answer to which we do not have access due to the conditions of uncertainty under which we live, but, rather, *Should we, as Christians seeking to live well in an uncertain world, base our lives, at least in part, on the conviction that God calls each one of us to accept certain specifiable roles or sets of responsibilities?* This question, I suggest (and you must decide whether and why you agree or disagree) captures the heart of what most of us who are concerned with vocation want to know, and does it in a way that honors what theology and faith are really all about.

The long form of this question is not something I want to write or you want to read on every other page. As a kind of shorthand, therefore, I will use the question, *Does God call us?* where the "us" is understood to refer to each individual Christian. You should remember, though, what we are really asking when we use that shorthand form. We are not, by this question, in either form, insisting on asking and answering questions about the reality that is beyond human knowing. However, in case anyone is tempted to think otherwise, we should not feel removed from the sense of awe I discussed earlier, for our question still asks us to decide on what we will base our lives.

Step Two: Why We Should Care

As I have suggested, spending some time pondering why we care about whether God calls us may not give us many insights into the theological question at hand (though, on the other hand, it might), but it can help us to gain the energy we need for intense theological exploration. It also helps us to be sure our minds and our hearts are both involved in the process.

Some of the reasons we do and should care about vocation are general ones that apply to most, if not all, Christians; others will be more specific to me or to you. One of the general reasons we want to know whether God is calling and what that means is that this is one way of trying to understand how God relates to human beings. (You understand at this point, of course, that any statement about what God does must be expanded into something like our long form of the vocation question.) Within Christianity, God is generally taken to be Creator, Redeemer, and Sustainer; each of these complex images tries to capture something of who God is and describes a relationship between God and us that has implications for the ways in which we live, and ought to live, our lives. In an equally powerful way, the notion that God calls us both depends upon a particular view of God and also is reflected in our behavior. Indeed, its possible implications for our lives are so important that we would be foolish not to figure out where we stand on it.

Part of figuring out where we stand requires us to be open to many possible answers, which is not always easy. For example, I sometimes have to remind myself not to dismiss too quickly someone who approaches me and asks whether I am "right with God" or whether I am saved. Although I admit to finding the strategy annoying, the fact is that the other person could be right and I could be wrong. Openness in matters of faith and theology, though without the assumption that all possible answers are equal, is a good thing. We should not lightly dismiss proposed answers to the question of our relationship with God or, in our case, to the question of whether and to what God might be calling us.

A second reason we should care about vocation is that the issues surrounding it fill Christian conversation. For example, the conviction that God is taking an active role in the world by doing such things as giving us certain gifts and leading us along certain career paths is commonplace in many Christian clusters. Thus, to explore the idea that God calls us is simultaneously to be exploring this active nature of God. Not only is the vocation issue worth caring about because Christians say such things as "this is not a job; it's my calling," but because of the many other activities we attribute to God. We tell one another that "it must have been his time to go" as a way of explaining an unanticipated death. Other unwanted events evoke the response that "everything happens for a reason." Many of us believe that God has set aside one person to be our lifelong marriage partner and that we will encounter this person when the time is right. We often speak of "God's plan" for the world or for individuals in it. All of these typical Christian ways of seeing the world draw on and express faith convictions that overlap to a greater or lesser extent with the convictions behind the idea of vocation. To clarify what we mean by vocation, therefore, helps us to understand and to reflect upon many common Christian ways of making sense of life.

A third reason it is worth investigating whether God calls is that in one way or another this issue encompasses many of the most interesting questions of Christian ethics (the examination of morality from within a Christian context). Although I have a particular interest here as a Christian ethicist, every Christian is concerned with one or more of the great ethical issues of our time. To say we are given responsibilities by God and that some of these may have to do with the primary roles of our lives may well have an impact on a myriad of issues, such as capital punishment, racism, abortion, economic justice, marriage, sexual behavior, family relationships, environmental responsibility, the rights of citizens, the privileges of leadership, and good stewardship. The number of ethical issues that overlap vocational ones should make any Christian consider carefully what vocation is all about, what theological claims lie behind it, and what an affirmation of these central claims would mean for our lives.

Why do I personally care about vocation? My attention to the idea of vocation was sparked by the Lilly Endowment's invitation to Hanover College in 1999 to apply for a grant in its Theological Exploration of Vocation initiative.[1] As the director of Hanover's Vocation

Project, I have had the privilege of working with hundreds of students and many professional colleagues as we, jointly and separately, explore what living vocationally in a Christian context is all about. This adventure has been both intellectually stimulating and spiritually engaging, and it has helped me to see how the many dimensions of a theological exploration of vocation can combine to positive effect in people's lives. The greater sense I can make of the idea that God calls to us, therefore, the more fully I can understand my own life and the more I can contribute to others as they work within a Christian context to live well. Finally, for all the good professional and theoretical reasons there are to explore the issue of whether God is calling and what God is saying, I just want to know. I was attracted to Christian ethics as a discipline because I wanted to know how I should live. The exploration of vocation appeals to me simply because discovering how to live our lives well before God and with one another is my single most pressing concern in life and has been for as long as I can remember. Does this have anything to do with the genetic and environmental influence of having a sometimes-perfectionist mother? I imagine so. Does it derive from experiencing pains and needs in myself and others to a perhaps exaggerated extent? From my longing for a more caring and just world? Probably. I need to keep these bits of autobiography in mind as I ponder whether God calls, but not to ponder this is not a possibility for me. Am I in the right job? Should I be doing this job differently? Am I treating others correctly? Am I acting rightly and faithfully as a brother, son, and uncle? How about in my friendships? Should I re-marry? Have I met the person I should re-marry? These are critical and often-present questions for me, and deep engagement with the issue of vocation is a way to seek their answers.

What about you? Why do you care whether or not God calls? Are you most interested in thinking about who God is? Are you pondering what you should do with your life? Are you wondering how to hear God's call to you? Before going on, pause for a moment to engage the question at this personal level.

Step Three: Developing a Hypothesis

Do you remember the long version of our question: *Should we, as Christians seeking to live well in an uncertain world, base our lives,*

at least in part, on the conviction that God calls each one of us to
accept certain specifiable roles or sets of responsibilities? As you
remember, moving from whatever our gut response is (mine is "yes")
to a more developed statement of our view is facilitated by looking at
three elements: presuppositions, meanings, and implications. As
questions, these would be: What is assumed in the question? What
do the key words or phrases mean? What would be the implications
of taking such a position? These elements can be considered by way
of a series of carefully constructed and critical questions.

You may have other critical questions in mind in order to move
from our question and gut response to our hypothesis. The ones that
follow are the ones that emerge for me as I consider what Christians
are likely to be assuming when they pose the vocation question or the
key terms and phrases that we must clarify if we really want to understand what we are asking or hypothesizing. We examine later the
implications of taking our position.

1. Do we have a relationship with God?
2. Is God personal?
3. Does God intervene in our lives?
4. Does God have a plan for us, collectively or individually?
5. Does God reveal how we should live?
6. Does God reveal our vocational roles?
7. What does it mean to talk about general and unique roles or
   responsibilities?
8. What does it mean to "call"?

You may notice that any one of these could be the central question
in a theological analysis. We might, for instance, have as our primary
concern the question of whether God intervenes in our lives. Our primary question would be something to do with God's intervention, and
we would need to articulate and respond to a series of critical questions, including some of the ones just listed, prior to reaching a
hypothesis. When we begin to articulate and analyze assumptions,
meanings, and implications, we find that most, if not all, theological
questions are interrelated. As you continue to push on your convictions and questions in order to identify where you stand, do not be
trapped into thinking that there are some statements or questions that
can only be seen as basic convictions and some that can only be seen

as critical questions about those convictions. Neither faith convictions nor theological investigation are that linear or that hierarchical.

What this means, of course, is that the most thorough exploration of the question of whether God calls us would require us to run through the entire process of theological analysis with each of the critical questions above. However, although valuable theological reflection never ends, this book must, so I need to take some shortcuts. One difficult decision we always face concerns which issues are pressing upon us for answers and with which ones we can take some reflective shortcuts. One way to separate crucial issues from subsidiary ones is to be aware of what is bubbling up into our consciousness, what is demanded in the moment by the actions and reactions of our daily lives, and what issues we are tempted to avoid, but should not, because they create problems for us intellectually, emotionally, or relationally.

As you try to sort out crucial questions on vocation from less important ones, you may find that your questions are rather different from the ones I identified above. As I briefly discuss each of the above questions, you should gain a deeper sense of how to explore your own questions. Spend some time analyzing your questions carefully and articulating answers that appear to give you insight into vocation.

1. Do We Have a Relationship with God?

In order to be able to accept a view that God calls us and that we hear and respond, we must first be able to take the position that some meaningful kind of relationship exists between us and God. I cannot answer for you the question of whether you take yourself to have a relationship with God, but certainly most Christians believe they do. One place to see this is in the practice of prayer, whether corporate or personal. For many Christians, including myself, prayer is a primary form of expressing the sense of relationship with God, which means that we can learn something about the way we think of God (and how, therefore, we might want to think of God calling us) by focusing on whether and how we pray. I think my views on and practice of prayer are very similar to those of many Christians, so I will spend some time looking at my own prayer history to see whether we can learn anything helpful about the God-Christian relationship. As I do, ponder what evidence exists in your own life for a position on the question of whether you have a relationship with God.

As far as I can remember, my prayer life has had three primary parts. I would be tempted to call these stages, but that would give the impression that one concluded as the next one appeared, whereas in fact they have often existed simultaneously and early forms still continue today. The first was reciting prayers at night that I had learned in church or from my parents. The second was frequently asking God to help me or guide me or support me or do something specific in my life or the life of someone I cared about. The third might best be called meditation or contemplative prayer.

In my nightly prayers, I often included one or more that I had learned from attending, and eventually serving as an acolyte in, my home Episcopal church. These included the Lord's Prayer, which I am pretty sure I had first been taught by my parents, and also other prayers that I had memorized through repetition. I remember, for example, repeating a communion prayer and a corporate confession, not because they expressed anything I wanted to express in faith to God, but because of their association with my church home and my feeling of the presence of God (and, surely, to some degree because I wanted to impress my parents with my memory). The fact that God was near and listening to me seemed much more important than anything I might say.

Although I have not spent much time memorizing prayers since I was young, there are still some that I repeat frequently when I am wandering around the world and want to feel connected with God. One is the Lord's Prayer, one of the most powerful and well-known Christian prayers. During one semester when I was preaching a sermon series on this prayer, I would repeat it over and over to myself when I took our dog, Zoe, for one of her daily walks around the campus. As this prayer sank more and more into my heart and mind, a certain transformation of attitude occurred that brightened my life. Most of you reading this book know this prayer; for those who do not, here is one of its major versions:

> Our Father, who art in heaven, hallowed be thy name,
> Thy kingdom come.
> Thy will be done on earth as it is in heaven.
> Give us this day our daily bread.
> And forgive us our trespasses, as we forgive those who trespass
>   against us.
> And lead us not into temptation, but deliver us from evil.

For thine is the kingdom, and the power, and the glory.
Forever and ever. Amen.

Three other prayers have played similar roles in my life, centering me on God and things of God in particular periods. One is the frequently cited prayer from early centuries of the church:

Almighty God,
to whom all hearts are open,
all desires, known,
and from whom no secrets are hid:
Cleanse the thoughts of our hearts
by the inspiration of your Holy Spirit,
that we may perfectly love you
and worthily magnify your holy name;
through Christ our Lord.[2]

A pastor friend of mine reminded me of this prayer once when we were discussing personalizing our spiritual practices. She used it as an example of something that had been meaningful to her. I have found that saying it slowly and with a vulnerable heart is helpful in reminding me of the presence of God.

One of the shortest of all prayers as well as one of the most frequently used in various parts of the church is the so-called Jesus prayer. It comes in a couple of versions, but one is simply, "Lord Jesus Christ, Son of God, have mercy upon me." When other words will not come, this can profoundly express one's heart.

Finally, while on retreats at Gethsemani Abbey, I have picked up these words that are often recited by the monks there as they begin their prayer times. The opening words echo Psalm 70, and they have been centering and refreshing for me on many occasions.

O God, come to my assistance.
O Lord, make haste to help me.
Praise the Father, the Son, and Holy Spirit,
both now and for ever,
the God who is, who was, and is to come, at the end of the ages.

The second major form of prayer in my life is prayers on behalf of someone, either myself or another. This kind of prayer will also be familiar to most Christians. I remember praying to God to help me do well on a test or in a basketball game or, later, in a gymnastics or track meet (as I recall, God was best at answering the latter prayers positively). I have prayed to God to get me out of one perceived fix or another, to help me to say the right thing, to help me help someone else, to speak through me in a sermon, to help me stay calm in stressful moments. I have prayed to God when people close to me were sick or in some other way troubled. From general prayers asking God to "bless Nana and Grandpa" to more specific ones later in life, these kinds of quick and often unrepeated prayers have always been a part of my prayer life. Today, I often name people whose needs are somehow brought to my attention and ask God to surround them with love, light, and healing.

It would require a long digression to sort out how we should think about these kinds of prayers, but I have been astonished in my life at some of the places they have worked. I have been equally astonished at some of the places they have not worked. I remember once in high school praying that a particular event would happen in a friend's life (any more information and the situation would be identifiable; it was a small high school!). One evening, while praying as hard as I could for this friend, I felt this rush of energy through my body, followed by a sense of assurance that what I had been praying for had been answered. As I found out the next day, it had, and right at the time I had my experience. On the other hand, there are some people and situations for whom or for which I have prayed time and time again and nothing ever seems to change. One can always say, of course, that sometimes God says yes and sometimes God says no, or that God always answers prayers but in God's own time and way, but these are faith convictions that demand their own theological exploration. They also, it seems to me, tend to make it impossible for us ever to see response to prayer as more than an exercise in randomness by God and, in the end, may make it impossible to say anything meaningful at all about prayer, since any moment may be described as a yes or no answer to someone or another's prayer.

As the years went by, one additional form of prayer became important to me: meditation. Although many Christians have discovered meditation through encounters with Eastern religious traditions such as Buddhism, Christianity has its own traditions of meditation.[3] I practiced forms of meditation and contemplative prayer for several years during my pastoral ministry; my assumption then was that these were a way to be fully present with God, to rest in God. I did not approach these times with petitions, but simply hoped to place myself in harmony with God. For whatever reasons, those practices attract me less these days, but they are one of the forms that my communication with God has taken over the years.

What is the relevance of this discussion of my prayer life to the theological question of whether God calls us? In this current stage of theological analysis, we are trying to formulate a hypothesis, a clearly stated faith conviction that can then be put in conversation with our partners in the next analytical step. Part of articulating this faith conviction clearly is to look at related ideas and practices in the lives of Christians to see what insight we might gain about vocation. Since to be called is to be in some kind of relationship with God, it is worth looking at other ways this sense of relationship is expressed. Insofar as my prayer life has been somewhat typical of most Christians, it reveals a sense or underlying belief that God is accessible to us and responsive to us. Most of us do not assume that God will always do what we want or that God is listening only to us, but the Christians I know certainly tend to believe and act in accordance with the view that God is in some sense present and ready to talk, listen, or be communed with, at any moment. This information can be factored into our classification of our view on calling.

As you may have noticed, I just sneaked into our discussion the notion that God is present to us. This idea is certainly a common one for those who pray, and it is important enough not to be sneaked into the conversation without some attention being paid to it. For some, the notion that God is present means little more than that God is somehow all around us, but for many it has a connotation of accessibility and comfort. As an example of the latter, some Christians say that God is "watching over" them. When I ask people what they mean by that, I typically hear either that God is protecting them or that God has a plan for them. That God protects Christians may be a claim about God carrying us into a rewarding afterlife, an issue well beyond the scope of this book. However, if it means that God doesn't let anything bad happen to faithful people in this life, then it is simply a false claim. If, on the other hand, it means something deeply metaphorical such as what is behind the expression, "God is always there to hold my hand, even when times are awful," it may come closer to what seems to me to be true. It does not, however, account for the common experience of God's absence, epitomized in the "why have you forsaken me?" experience of Jesus on the cross.

Some skeptics respond to all of this discussion about the presence of God, prayer, and having a relationship with God by saying that these ideas are based on psychological need and are, therefore, simply false. The critically thinking theologian must not shrink from the same skeptical wondering. Do you recognize the relevant need in yourself? I am pretty sure I recognize it in me. Still, I find that there are good reasons for rejecting the typically offered conclusions of this kind of skeptical view; by naming them, we can learn something about theology in the process.

The origin of a particular conviction or claim does not guarantee anything about its truth or its falsity. Our need to believe that our parents love us, for instance, is not a guarantee that they do or that they do not. A professor's need to blame anything that goes wrong in one of his courses on the people who published the books he used, the people who trained him in his field, the administration that required him to serve on a committee that semester, or the students in the class does not guarantee that anyone but he is responsible for messing up the course. Again, suppose someone goes through life needing to believe that things are going to get better than they are, or that her cat ran away instead of being hit in the road, or that unicorns are the defenders of heaven. Any of these beliefs might be true or false, but their truth is independent of one's need to believe them.

The person of faith who is practicing good theological analysis will ask a different question than this one about the origins of belief, namely, *Do we have good reasons for committing ourselves to the view that one or another type of relationship with God is ongoing in our lives?* Even if the correlation between a psychological need and a particular faith conviction does not negate the conviction, it is equally true that neither the need nor any other autobiographical fact in and of itself guarantees the truth of the conviction. That said, our need does provide at least one reason for committing oneself to a particular faith stance. Faith and theology, as discussed in earlier chapters, are resources for living well in the world. To that end, one of the ways in which we assess any given theological conviction is by its ability to enable individuals and communities to live better lives, where "better" includes such things as reaching out in love to others. Commitment to the idea that we Christians have an ongoing relationship with God provides us with the ability to live richer and better lives. Of course, some ways of understanding God might contribute more than others to our goal of living well. It might well be the case, for example, that committing oneself to the view that one is in an ongoing relationship with a loving God is quite different from committing oneself to an ongoing relationship with a punishing God from whom one cannot escape. For now, as we search for where we stand on this question of whether we have a relationship with God, our conclusion can simply be that the nature of Christian prayer practices, including mine and probably yours, indicates a deep and widespread conviction that God is in some sense present to us and that some kind of communication in both directions is possible. Appeal to common practices is not a final appeal (after all, many practices are common but based on false assumptions), but it is important for getting our critical work under way and for beginning to establish a testable conviction.

2. Is God Personal?

Is this relationship we have with God a personal one? If you walk into any Christian worship service with this question in mind, you are likely to come away with the idea that God is like a person in certain specifiable ways. You will hear all the intentions, emotions, and activities ascribed to God that are usually ascribed to people, though typically in magnified or even absolute ways: God does not just know a lot; God knows everything. God is not just able to do some things; God is able to do anything and everything. God is not simply able to make stuff; God created the whole world (and, in this case, did it out of nothing, something no one else can do). God is not just righteous and just, but is or provides the very definition of these concepts. It is easy to caricature these claims: God is a lot like all of your favorite superheroes put together, a human being magnified to the nth degree. On the other hand, these convictions are widespread, far beyond Christianity and Christian history, and cannot be dismissed with a quick caricature.

For some people, including some Christians, one of the stumbling blocks to faith appears to be the ancient idea that God is some kind of super person. It is worth reflecting on whether it is possible to have a personal relationship with God even if God is not personlike. It is worth asking to what extent a commitment to the personhood (or superhumanity) of God is necessary for contemporary Christians and the well-being of the world. Can a relationship have certain "personal" qualities about it even if one of the two partners in the relationship is not a person? I think so. Many things can affect us deeply, including a solitary walk in the woods, petting our cat or dog, gazing at the ocean, solving a difficult problem, meditating on the idea of love, and hearing Bach's "Little Fugue in G Minor." We can find peace, inspiration, clarity, excitement, grief, and many other states of being through interactions with "others" that are non-personlike. These reflections seem to suggest that using the language of personal relationship when referring to that which is not personlike can be appropriate.

This is not a radically new idea, and it continues to be explored by various Christian theologians who find the notion of a personlike God to be problematic. Note that there are two directions we might take in thinking about it. We might assume, for whatever reasons, that we have some kind of relationship with God and then ask whether there can be a personal relationship with that which is nonpersonal. Or we might start with the notion that God is nonpersonal and then ponder what sort of relationship we might have with such a God. Since I started by discussing whether we have a relationship with God, I have led us into the first of these directions, but it is not the only possible one.

3. Does God Intervene in Our Lives?

Another issue that intersects with the question of whether God calls is whether God intervenes in our lives. The notion that God calls seems, on the face of it, to suggest a God who intervenes, who goes in and out of our lives when appropriate, pointing us in one direction rather than another. As part of clarifying where we should stand on the notion that God calls us, it may be helpful to clarify what it might mean to say that God intervenes.

As at so many points in our journey, it is important here to look to your own life for guidance. We always start with where we are and what we think today. What have our experiences been, and to what view have they led us? We will often not end in this place, but our own experiences and decisions provide us with a place to start on each question. Do you have experiences of God intervening in your life?

Do you have experiences of needing God to intervene but receiving no response?

My own reflection begins with the memory of one evening in Virginia. I was kneeling at the altar crying and asking God for help. God did not do anything. Well, okay, maybe God did something, but I had and have no reason to suppose so. No problem was solved, nothing felt better, and there was no communication from God that I could recognize as such. I eventually just got up and went home. One might say that my ability to go home was God's work. One might say that the fact that I am no longer crying at the altar is God's work. One might say any number of such things, but outside of such seemingly arbitrary assertions, I do not have any good reasons for affirming that God intervened in my life that night or, with respect to the issue that was troubling me, in the days following. At the same time, there have been occasions when I clearly felt as though God was intervening. The rush I felt praying for my high school friend is one instance. The healing that took place as I meditated before the icon is another. Were I to base my view solely on my impressions in these kinds of instances, impressions that are themselves based upon being taught to name some events and feelings as God's work, I would say that sometimes God intervenes in our lives and sometimes, even though asked, God does not.

There are some temptations we face in thinking about God's intervention. One, already mentioned, is the hasty move to the view that God is personlike. Another is the unfortunate tendency to use God simply as an explanation. A third is to suppose that denying that or questioning whether God intervenes implies a lack of gratitude on our part. But giving God thanks is quite appropriate, regardless of our decisions about God's episodic intervention in our lives.

We are too often tempted to appeal to God as the "explanation" for what we cannot otherwise understand. Here, though, I mean explanation in a particular sense. After all, this book is premised in part on the view that commitment to some version of the Christian understanding of God is an appropriate way to make sense of the world; if giving an explanation is simply a matter of making sense of something, then it seems appropriate to see God as an explanation. However, God should not be made the *causal* explanation (or "efficient cause") for that for which we cannot otherwise account. For example, a healing happens that medicine cannot explain and we say, "It must be God." We say that the world is here because God created it. We explain unexpected deaths, great triumphs, bad things happening to bad people, good things happening to good people, jobs we get and jobs we do not get, the presence of humankind on the Earth, and virtually everything else by saying "God did it." This is a mistake. For one thing, we can never be certain about such things. For another, it threatens to make God smaller and smaller as other explanations, primarily scientific ones, emerge. What does it mean for us when we have said that God miraculously restored someone's health, but then our physician finds a medical reason? For a third, this kind of reasoning encourages an illegitimate blending of science and theology into attempts to discern cause-and-effect relationships; this is certainly not the point of theology. When people of faith claim that God is the way they make sense of the world, because, without God, they would not know how to explain some mysterious occurrences, they threaten the true role of God in the faith of the Christian. We miss the point when God becomes a causal explanation instead of the heart of our orientation to the world, the reference point by which we locate all that we are and all that we do.

To say that God should not be used as a causal explanation is not to say that God does not, in fact, intervene, but it may suggest that we should resist making interventionist claims that are primarily causal. It is quite appropriate to say that God created the world or God gave me peace when I am expressing or advocating the humble and thankful orientation that Christians should have to the world, yet to say either of these things as a way of literally explaining how they occurred is not appropriate. It misses the point of faith and theology and also fails to meet any reasonable conditions for specifying causality. In the claim that God intervenes, we hear the reminder that we are not in charge. What we have and who we are, and even that we are, comes to us as a gift.

To say that God intervenes also implies a reduction in human freedom. As we discussed earlier, a key feature of our humanity is that we must make choices. We never want to ignore the extent to which some in our world have an illegitimately wider range within which to choose than others do, but we typically think negatively about restricting free choice on the grounds that it limits one's humanity. To the extent that we impute choice and intervention to God, we limit human choices, as God's intervention in one situation is likely to have a ripple effect in many other situations. Imagine how extensively God might have to manipulate the world in order to bring you together with the one you are supposed to marry, for instance. Consider the limitations inherent in shaping your choice and her or his choice of where to go to college, or perhaps your parents' choices about careers that will enable them to pay for that school. The extent of the limitations on free choice that might be required in some such instances appears to me to be a high cost for everyone else to pay in order to match you or any one of us with the right spouse. This example may be more absurd than is necessary, but I hope it makes the point clear.

The problem of suffering may also make us hesitant to argue that God intervenes in our lives. Indeed, the apparent arbitrariness of suffering seems to me to be the most devastating critique of most typical Christian ways of thinking about an interventionist God. Even where we are able to predict suffering, it is typically more a matter of statistics, of causal explanation, than of really understanding why such a thing would happen to this person in this place, particularly if there is a God who cares and can do something about it. Again, what we are pondering here is not the fact of whether God intervenes (for we do not have access to that), but the appropriateness of this view for our theological vision. About all we can say about whether God really intervenes is that we are uncertain, but for our theological views we have to say that it is a difficult notion to accept, even if our experience and the Christian tradition are filled with examples. How can we commit ourselves to an understanding of God that includes apparently arbitrary intervention, where one person lives and one person dies, one person suffers and one person rejoices, one person is born in poverty and one person is born in great wealth.[4] There seems to be no way to make sense of these things other than to say God must have reasons that are hidden from us. Neither of those strikes me as theologically adequate. We would at least have to explore this very carefully before deciding it was the best view for this hurting world to take.

Can we hold a view of vocation without intervention? The idea that we should not make interventionist claims will make most Christians cringe. After all, much of the heart of Christianity is based on the idea that God comes into history, that God intervenes. To be honest, I do not particularly want to have reservations about saying that God intervenes in our lives. We shall see where these reflections take us; if the assumption that God intervenes contributes significantly to or is necessary for us to have attitudes of humility and gratitude, then we may have good reasons for holding onto it. If not, then we may come to find that the notion that God intervenes is one we need to be courageous enough to reject. In either case, we will be right in taking great care before committing ourselves to either model.

4. Does God Have a Plan for Us, Collectively or Individually?

Though in many ways a version of the interventionist understanding of God, and therefore not meriting extended discussion here, one of the most frequently uttered and widespread claims in Christian discourse these days is the claim that at least some things that occur are part of "God's plan." In the classroom, I hear this said in a variety of ways: "I know that if I can just be patient, God will show me the right direction for my life." "God has a plan for each one of us." "I guess I'll go to heaven if it's part of God's plan." "Everything happens for a reason." "God must have wanted him in heaven; that's why he died." "If it's God's plan for me to marry someone, then God will bring us together at the right time."

The notion that God has a plan for us certainly fits well with some ideas of vocation, but our discussion of the notion that God intervenes suggests that it may be difficult to fit God's plans and human freedom together into a coherent point of view. If God's plan must come to fruition, then God must have created things in such a way or be currently shaping things in such a way that not all choices are, ultimately, possible. The more specific we make elements of this plan, the more freedom we lose. Since so many events are inextricably connected, as we discussed in chapter 2, requiring that one of them work out in a certain way will mean giving shape to many of them. After a bit of reflection on this, we have to wonder whether conceiving of the world in this fashion would mean that God has to be in control of everything that happens everywhere. What do you think of that point of view?

5. Does God Reveal How We Should Live?

There appear to be four general attitudes people take with respect to God's control over our lives. One is that God has set up virtually everything to happen the way God wants it to happen. God has already made it the case that I will say certain specific things in the third class period of my introductory theology course this semester. The second is that God just determines the major events in our lives and we control the rest. God has made me a teacher; the rest is up to me. The third is that God does not control anything except for the outcome of whether we are saved or damned. Whether I teach or do not teach, whether I feed the poor or ignore them, the final outcome will be the same. The last is that God created the world and then leaves us to our own devices. We are here; the rest is up to us.

Typically, views that include some degree of human freedom to make decisions and to act on them also include norms given by God to guide those decisions and actions. Christians describe these in a number of ways, ranging from strong suggestions to absolute demands; always, though, they tell us how we are to live, and they are said to come from God. To say that God reveals something to us seems to imply that we believe that God intervenes in our lives. Christians are typically convinced that God reveals some norms (Exod. 20:16: "You shall not bear false witness against your neighbor") even if human beings come up with others on their own ("No right on red"). However, we have seen some reasons to wonder whether the idea that God intervenes is one we should hold. Now, if we want to put intervention, and thus revelation, aside, can we still say there are some norms that are not created by human beings?

You remember that a major reason we hesitated about affirming the idea that God intervenes was because it is so often used as a way to talk about causes and effects. Suppose we say that there are norms that human beings do not create, but simply set aside for the moment the question of from where these norms originate. This approach would mean that you and I experience some things as given but would not require us to explain them as directly given by God. We could say, for instance, that they are just built into the world. To put it another way, there simply are guidelines present to us, rather like the air we breathe, that demand our attention.

6. Does God Reveal Our Vocational Roles?

From the answers to the previous few questions, you have almost everything you need to answer this question without any comments from me. How would you answer it? What are the pieces of the question you would pull out to reflect on immediately?

You might have focused on "vocational roles" or even on "God," but my choice would be "reveal." We have just pointed out how careful we need to be about attributing direct revelation to God. At the same time, we have said that we experience some norms as simply given to us. What, if anything, would this lead us to say in response to question six? Can vocational roles, such as work, family relationships, or congregational membership, be given to us? Can these somehow be built into the world?

Christian testimony through the ages and the contemporary experiences of many Christians seem to suggest this possibility. As we will see in the next chapter, both the understanding and the experience of certain vocational roles as given to us are common in Christian circles. The experience is often described in expressions such as "I just couldn't do anything else with my life" or "Honor your father and mother." The understanding is an interpretation of these experiences that sees them as offered to us or mandated for us, with some level of decision on our part being needed if we are going to fulfill them completely.

These roles might be characterized as collections of norms. In some sense, to consider a certain career a calling is to accept a whole set of right and wrong ways to live. If ministry is one's calling, then the list of things one is supposed to do—including preaching the gospel, visiting the sick, and pointing people to God—is clear, even if the details of how to execute these responsibilities require additional discernment. If we put all of the "oughts" together, though, we essentially build a calling. Granted, this is not a very romantic way of thinking about one's vocation and probably distorts much of what the called person sees himself or herself as doing in a given day or week. However, if we do not allow this understanding to result in a joyless perfectionism, we can seek our callings with the assurance that guidance follows.

If you think the previous paragraph or two are not very promising in terms of their ability to make sense of the idea that God calls to us, read through the ideas again and pause to think about them carefully. What is it, exactly, that you find to be confusing or bothersome? What do you find to be appropriate or helpful? How would you amend my suggestions to make them fit more closely with your own responses to the question of whether God calls? Pausing to sort this out now will pay dividends as we move through our remaining chapters.

7. What Does It Mean to Talk about General and Unique Roles or Responsibilities?

From our personal experiences, we can all affirm that there are certain responsibilities and roles that appear to be unique to us and other ones that appear to be more general. As an example of general responsibilities, most of us who have been raised in the West tend to think that all human beings have certain moral obligations or, at least, face certain moral prohibitions that are absolute, such as rape and torture. More uniquely, we view many of our roles as chosen but think there are various responsibilities that automatically become part of anyone's life once they are in those roles. You may choose to be a mother or father, but once you are in that role, you must do certain things for the well-being of your child or children. You may choose whether or not to be a member of a church, but once you are a member, you should and should not act in certain ways relative to the views of your church. There are also unchosen roles, such as being a daughter or a son, that impose various responsibilities on us. At this stage of our analysis, simply recognize the extent to which we can capture many of the similarities and differences between two people by specifying their differing responsibilities and roles.

8. What Does It Mean to "Call"?

The notion of calling typically invokes certain images for us. The one I see first is someone standing and ringing a dinner bell, wanting us to come in for dinner. If, though, we want to suspend judgment for the moment on whether God is personlike, has intentions, is a being, or intervenes in our lives, this meaning of God calling would be difficult to maintain.

Still, though, we return time and again to this sense we have that we are faced with givens in life, that we are urged forward by the universe somehow, that the universe poses questions to us in each moment about how we will respond, that some ways of living are right for us and some are not right for us. Does it make sense to refer to these things as God's call without being sure that God is an intentional Caller? We are typically attracted to the idea that God is somehow involved in these experiences, but many of us also find it difficult to affirm all of the characteristics of God and God's involvement in our lives that are typically attached to these experiences. We will move toward a way to deal with this dilemma by stating our hypothesis carefully and then testing it diligently with our conversation partners.

Step Three Continued: A Hypothesis

We began trying to formulate our hypothesis with this question: *should we, as Christians seeking to live well in an uncertain world, base our lives, at least in part, on the conviction that God calls each one of us to accept certain specifiable roles or sets of responsibilities?* You and I may have arrived at different conclusions at this point, and it is important for you to recognize and articulate any differences between us in your formulation of a hypothesis. What neither of us can avoid, however, is taking into account our brief critical explorations in our formulation. Remember, we are in the process of constructing a theological point of view, a stance we can take that will guide our lives and that we can recommend to other Christians as worthy of exploration, at least, and commitment, at best. We cannot know at this point where our investigation will end up, but we are about to offer our best shot to the partners for conversation.

We have already come a long way in our theological exploration. We have seen a certain givenness to human life—certain characteristics each one of us has, sometimes in common and sometimes uniquely—that are the context within which we choose what we will do and who we will be. We have also seen, from the very first chapter, that one way to understand how we face the world is that the universe is continually posing questions to us about how we will respond: "What will you do now?" it seems to ask. We have also noted an experience many of us have that various responsibilities or norms for how we should live seem to come to us from reality itself; we can feel their tug, as it were, and sense ourselves as being more deeply responsible for following them than if we were convinced it were simply our society, our family, or our peers leading us.

We have seen that we Christians typically take ourselves to have some kind of relationship with God (though we understand God in many different ways), a relationship that expresses itself in such practices as prayer. We have characterized this sense of relationship as including the view that God is accessible to us and responsive to us in some way. We have distinguished between the notion of a personlike God and a God who is not personlike, but with whom we can still have a personal relationship in the sense that we are deeply engaged and affected by it. We have puzzled over whether and how it makes sense to say that God intervenes or that God has a plan for us or that God reveals things to us. What, now, does it look like to put all of this together? What is the reality we want to explore behind the notion that God calls?

I propose that when we say God calls us we should mean something like the following. This hypothesis is not, obviously, a scientifically testable one, so we should not be misled by the word, but it is a statement of conviction that we can explore in conversation with our partners: *We experience much of who we are and much of our world as given to us and as demanding response from us. Among the givens we experience are various norms (some asked of all of us and some more unique), some of which appear to be or to relate to vocations. There are certain signals we can use to discern whether or not we are responding to the universe correctly. We tend to see God as the source of these norms, but we recognize problems with that understanding. We believe we live better lives, lives more likely to benefit the world, when we view our lives and experiences in these ways.*

You have been doing theological work for several chapters now. You have developed some skills in thinking about theological issues and questions. How do you evaluate this hypothesis? Do you agree with it or disagree with it? Does it accurately reflect what we have said to this point? Where would you like to amend it prior to entering into conversation with our partners? If your version differs from the one above, go ahead and write it here:

Notes

In the next chapter, we place our conviction(s) on the table for discussion among some of the many voices that can be heard in our conversation partners, attempting to discern whether what we have said fits within the parameters they set and learning from them additional details about how God's calls are sensed and understood. By the end of our journey, we will know a great deal more about both vocation and ourselves. We will better know how to discuss theologically the issue of vocation. We will see what it means to discern what God is calling us to do, and we will be able to use the discernment process in our own lives.

Questions for Reflection

1. Do you experience aspects of your life as given to you instead of chosen by you? What are some examples?
2. Have you thought about what you are called to do? What have you discerned so far? What was your process of discernment?
3. Does God call us? How would you draw out the meaning of the word "call"?
4. I discussed several questions in the "Developing a Hypothesis" section of this chapter. Which one did you find most provocative, challenging, or disturbing? Why? What is your current answer to the question?
5. Most Christians think of God as personal. Do you? If so, what do you mean by "personal," and why do you think this is a good characterization of God? Could you worship a God who was not personal?
6. Are there parts of the hypothesis I have offered with which you cannot agree? If not, why not? If so, how would you rewrite the hypothesis to better characterize your view of the same issues?

6

Vocation, Part 2: Conversations

We experience much of who we are and much of our world as given to us and as demanding response from us. Among the givens we experience are various norms (some asked of all of us and some more unique), some of which appear to be or to relate to vocations. There are certain signals we can use to discern whether or not we are responding to the universe correctly. We tend to see God as the source of these norms, but we recognize problems with that understanding. We believe we live better lives, lives more likely to benefit the world, when we view our lives and experiences in these ways.

E arlier, in order to help us to navigate our way through complicated material, we used the statement "God calls us" as a shorthand version of a longer claim. The length and complexity of our hypothesis lends itself to the same strategy. Here is a shorthand version to guide us through this chapter: *God is continually calling to us. We can discern and follow God's leading.*

Notice the significant difference between these two statements aside from their length. "God" is the subject of the first part of the shorthand version, but "we" is the subject of each of the many parts of the detailed version. You should already have an idea about what is happening here, but the final chapter will make it plain. Until then, you can rest assured that the tension between the two can be resolved.

In order to help us decide whether our hypothesis is an appropriate faith conviction, we are now going to enter into conversation with the multiple partners of Christianity. Beginning with the Bible, I briefly introduce each of the partners and examine a piece of what they have to say about vocation. With six partners to engage, you should take a break here and there as you work your way through this chapter. Examining this material carefully will pay off in the end, but there is a lot of it, and you will be able to think more clearly about it if you take occasional breaks.

The Bible: Old Testament

Reading the Bible is no easy task. When theologian Stanley Hauerwas suggests, in *Unleashing the Scripture*, that the Bible should be taken "out of the hands of individual Christians in North America," he points to a serious problem, or set of them, even though his solution may appear drastic.[1] Hauerwas's concerns are different from my own (he is focused on questions of "spiritual and moral transformation" and the authority of the church), but we can certainly agree that most of us should be more humble than we usually are in making claims about what the Bible says and how it is relevant to our lives. We should be reluctant to pick up the Bible, read a sentence or passage, and simply assume that we understand its meaning. To head in a different direction than Hauerwas, I would say that Christians have made numerous recommendations through the ages on how to hear God's voice in or through the biblical texts, and our task here is to examine why we are interpreting it the way we are and to be sure that our approaches to interpretation are consistent each time we read.

To be faithful to what I have just said, I need to say something about my own reading of the Bible. I take it that God's voice can be heard through the multiple voices in the Bible, though not every voice there is God's voice, even when the Bible claims that it is. The Bible is a collection of interpreted faith experiences of the faith ancestors of modern Jews and Christians and Muslims as they made their way through many centuries of history. Since their composition, the biblical stories, laws, and visions have guided these traditions, sometimes successfully and sometimes unsuccessfully, through these years and continue to be a major touch point for the traditions today. Because the text is so rich and varied, meditation on the Bible's words is frequently the best resource Christians have for encountering God in the modern day.

As I said, I take the Bible to contain multiple voices, not just one. God did not write each word of it; it is not straightforwardly the words of God, though it may be taken, appropriately and metaphorically, as the Word of God. It is not Paul's voice we hear in Psalms (it may not even be Paul's voice we hear in some of the Pauline Epistles); it is not the voice of the author of the early chapters of Isaiah that we hear in 1 Timothy; it is not God's voice we read directly in either place. My intention in selecting a few passages for us to explore is not to close off voices, but to make voices heard. I am, however, focusing on passages that occurred to me as I was thinking about where God seems to be calling someone. You may well think of additional examples, some of which point in a different direction, which will make your own exploration here even richer.

We are going to look at four passages from the Old Testament and three from the New Testament. I set the context very briefly for each one and give the translation of the text from the NRSV (New Revised Standard Version). Go to your Bible and read the chapters around these texts, as well as some commentary on the relevant biblical books, in order to have the fullest sense of what is happening. Each passage is quite remarkable in and of itself, apart from the purpose to which I am about to put it.

The first passage is from the Bible's first book, Genesis. The great stories of creation, fall, and the flood are among those that precede it. God's original purposes for creation failed through the sins of human beings, so God takes a different approach. Whether the Abram story is historical in the sense that it actually occurred to an identifiable person in an identifiable place at an identifiable time is doubtful; however, it conveys a powerful theological understanding of Israel's emergence from an encounter with God. The end of chapter 11 and the beginning of chapter 12 give us the genealogical steps from Shem, Noah's son, to the son of Terah, Abram, whose name will be changed by God to Abraham in 17:5.

> Now the LORD said to Abram, "Go from your country and
> your kindred and your father's house to the land that I will

show you. I will make of you a great nation, and I will bless
you, and make your name great, so that you will be a blessing. I will bless those who bless you, and the one who curses
you I will curse; and in you all the families of the earth shall
be blessed." So Abram went, as the LORD had told him; and
Lot went with him. (Gen. 12:1–4a)

The second passage is found in Exodus, a book whose title comes
from its major story, the freeing of the Hebrew people from slavery
in Egypt over three thousand years ago. Whether or not this exodus
happened as a historical event, the story is a formative one in Israel's
life and has become a model for the modern school of theology called
liberation theology. The central figure in the adventure is Moses, and
this passage is one of his encounters with God.

Moses was keeping the flock of his father-in-law Jethro, the
priest of Midian; he led his flock beyond the wilderness, and
came to Horeb, the mountain of God. There the angel of the
LORD appeared to him in a flame of fire out of a bush; he
looked, and the bush was blazing, yet it was not consumed.
Then Moses said, "I must turn aside and look at this great
sight, and see why the bush is not burned up." When the
LORD saw that he had turned aside to see, God called to him
out of the bush, "Moses, Moses!" And he said, "Here I am."
Then he said, "Come no closer! Remove the sandals from
your feet, for the place on which you are standing is holy
ground." He said further, "I am the God of your father, the
God of Abraham, the God of Isaac, and the God of Jacob."
And Moses hid his face, for he was afraid to look at God.
Then the LORD said, "I have observed the misery of my people who are in Egypt; I have heard their cry on account of
their taskmasters. Indeed, I know their sufferings. . . . So
come, I will send you to Pharaoh to bring my people, the
Israelites, out of Egypt." But Moses said to God, "Who am I
that I should go to Pharaoh, and bring the Israelites out of
Egypt?" (Exod. 3:1–7, 10–11)

The third passage is from a book of the Bible that is read much less
frequently, and many of its stories are less well known. First Samuel

is the beginning of a story that describes, theologically, Israel's transition to a monarchy under David. Preceding and accompanying the monarchy through its history are figures who continually try to call Israel to faith in God. One of these is Samuel.

> Now the boy Samuel was ministering to the LORD under Eli. The word of the LORD was rare in those days; visions were not widespread. At that time Eli, whose eyesight had begun to grow dim so that he could not see, was lying down in his room; the lamp of God had not yet gone out, and Samuel was lying down in the temple of the LORD, where the ark of God was. Then the LORD called, "Samuel! Samuel!" and he said, "Here I am!" and ran to Eli, and said, "Here I am, for you called me." But he said, "I did not call; lie down again." So he went and lay down. The LORD called again, "Samuel!" Samuel got up and went to Eli, and said, "Here I am, for you called me." But he said, "I did not call, my son; lie down again." Now Samuel did not yet know the LORD, and the word of the LORD had not yet been revealed to him. The LORD called Samuel again, a third time. And he got up and went to Eli, and said, "Here I am, for you called me." Then Eli perceived that the LORD was calling the boy. Therefore Eli said to Samuel, "Go, lie down; and if he calls you, you shall say, 'Speak, LORD, for your servant is listening.'" So Samuel went and lay down in his place. Now the LORD came and stood there, calling as before, "Samuel! Samuel!" And Samuel said, "Speak, for your servant is listening." (1 Sam. 3:1–10)

The final Old Testament passage that we will explore is the calling of the prophet Jeremiah. The story is set in Judah, the southern kingdom of the people of Israel, in the sixth century BCE. Jeremiah is called by God to challenge the practices of the political and religious powers of his day; his words, God's words, are not heeded, and Jerusalem falls to the Babylonians in 587/586 BCE.

> Now the word of the LORD came to me saying, "Before I formed you in the womb I knew you, and before you were born I consecrated you; I appointed you a prophet to the nations." Then I said, "Ah, Lord GOD! Truly I do not know

> how to speak, for I am only a boy." But the LORD said to me,
> "Do not say, 'I am only a boy'; for you shall go to all to whom
> I send you, and you shall speak whatever I command you. Do
> not be afraid of them, for I am with you to deliver you, says
> the LORD." Then the LORD put out his hand and touched my
> mouth; and the LORD said to me, "Now I have put my words
> in your mouth. See, today I appoint you over nations and over
> kingdoms, to pluck up and to pull down, to destroy and to
> overthrow, to build and to plant." (Jer. 1:4–10)

Now that we have listened to four voices from the Bible, we should pause and see where we stand in the investigation of our hypothesis. As you remember, this is what we are exploring: *God is continually calling to us. We can discern and follow God's leading.* Does that fit with what we have just read? Where would our hypothesis challenge the stories, and where would the stories challenge our hypothesis?

First, there is no doubt in any of these passages that God is seen as calling. As the people of Israel tell a part of their story, it is clear that they understand God to be in charge of these significant moments of the process. God is the one in control, shaping history through the naming of certain people to certain roles and responsibilities. God appears in certain lives at unpredictable moments and calls people to new ways of being. God uproots Abram and sends him to a new land, with promises to do remarkable things when Abram obeys. God surprises Moses with flames that are not consuming a bush in their midst, and Moses finds himself sent on a mission he obviously neither imagined for himself nor thinks he has the ability to accomplish. Though "the word of the LORD was rare in [Samuel's] days," God does come to Samuel and sets him on the road to a very different kind of life. God has an extended conversation with Jeremiah about their relationship and Jeremiah's task. God is clearly a Caller in a normal sense of the word in these passages.

How do the four characters in these stories discern God's call? There are differences among the passages. We are given no clue about Abram's discernment process; God just appears, tells him what to do, and Abram does it. We can imagine that he felt some overwhelming emotions—perhaps awe, shock, disbelief, terror, humility, or pride—at this interruption to his day, but we do not hear about that. Moses' process is different: he initially responds to the flaming bush with amazement and curiosity. He then responds to God with fear and self-doubt. What is fascinating about the Samuel case is that he has to be educated in the process of hearing God. He does not recognize God's voice and has to be told by Eli that it is God who is calling to him. It is well worth pondering, as we do later, to what extent education in hearing must play a part in our own discernment processes. Finally, Jeremiah does not seem to be particularly surprised that he and God are chatting, but he certainly doubts that he can do what God wants.

We know from the more complete biblical stories that God accompanies and guides Abram/Abraham, Moses, Samuel, and Jeremiah on their journeys. God does not leave them to face their tasks alone. The biblical authors saw God as intimately involved in the life of the people of Israel because of their importance for fulfilling God's purposes. Not only can God's call be discerned, therefore, but God enables us to do whatever it is God calls us to do.

There are at least three places where our shorthand hypothesis and these biblical stories would challenge one another. First, we do not know from these passages whether God was seen as a "continual" caller, as our shorthand hypothesis affirms. We see God intervening strategically to accomplish God's purposes, but these biblical stories offer no sense that God is calling to people in every moment. Second, we would have to provide some additional argument to add ourselves into the biblical picture. Perhaps God called Abram, Moses, Samuel, and Jeremiah, but that does not mean that God calls you and me. Third, the Bible presents a challenge with God's characteristics, for the God of these passages has many human traits. God converses, God cares about at least some suffering people, God hears, and God observes. Earlier, we raised questions about attributing human characteristics to God, so this would be another point where we would have to challenge and be challenged by our biblical partner. We will keep these three challenges in mind for later.

The Bible: New Testament

For the next passage, the first of three in the New Testament, consider a story about Jesus from Mark's Gospel. I have said that a defining mark for Christianity is the centrality of Jesus to the spiritual life. What makes Jesus so important for Christians, as you know, is that the church claims he is the incarnation (God becoming a human being) of the second person of the Trinity (the three persons—Creator, Redeemer, and Comforter—as one God). Even if you have questions about these tricky doctrines, stories such as this one from Mark can be understood as expressing the intimate relationship all Christians believe Jesus has to God, even if Christians describe the details of that relationship in different ways. Essentially, a Jesus who calls, commands, or instructs is, by Christian definition, calling, commanding, or instructing for or as God.

Mark is the shortest of the four Gospels and the one that is usually accepted to be the first one written, probably a few decades after Jesus' time. A Gospel is a sharing of the good news that is given to human beings in the person and message of Jesus. The Gospels are intensely theological works, not biographical ones. There is little attempt in them to detail the life of Jesus in a historical way; rather, the Gospel writers are attempting to make a case for his role as the Christ, the chosen one of God. This story from Mark is about a man's encounter with Jesus, Jesus' call to him to follow, and the man's struggle with the call.

> As he was setting out on a journey, a man ran up and knelt before him, and asked him, "Good Teacher, what must I do to inherit eternal life?" Jesus said to him, "Why do you call me good? No one is good but God alone. You know the commandments: 'You shall not murder; You shall not commit adultery; You shall not steal; You shall not bear false witness; You shall not defraud; Honor your father and mother.'" He said to him, "Teacher, I have kept all these since my youth." Jesus, looking at him, loved him and said, "You lack one thing; go, sell what you own, and give the money to the poor, and you will have treasure in heaven; then come, follow me." When he heard this, he was shocked and went away grieving, for he had many possessions. (Mark 10:17–22)

Certainly some of us hope that the young man had a change of heart and did as Jesus instructed, but the story does not tell us this. In its context, it is perhaps meant to provide an example of what it takes to receive the kingdom as a little child, as per Mark 10:15, and certainly sets up the challenging teachings on wealth that follow it.

The sixth biblical voice is from the book of Acts. Acts is the story of the birth and early development of the church. This passage is one account of Paul's conversion. He was, as Saul, a persecutor of Christians, but he became both a follower of Christ and the church's first great theologian.

> Now as [Saul] was going along and approaching Damascus, suddenly a light from heaven flashed around him. He fell to the ground and heard a voice saying to him, "Saul, Saul, why do you persecute me?" He asked, "Who are you, Lord?" The reply came, "I am Jesus, whom you are persecuting. Now get up and enter the city, and you will be told what you are to do." (Acts 9:3–6)

Finally, consider the following passage from the letter to the Ephesians. The text is addressed to Christians and sets their required activity in the context of God's purposes in the cosmos.

> I therefore, the prisoner in the Lord, beg you to lead a life worthy of the calling to which you have been called, with all humility and gentleness, with patience, bearing with one another in love, making every effort to maintain the unity of the Spirit in the bond of peace. There is one body and one Spirit, just as you were called to the one hope of your calling, one Lord, one faith, one baptism, one God and Father of all, who is above all and through all and in all. But each of us was given grace according to the measure of Christ's gift. Therefore it is said, "When He ascended on high he made captivity itself a captive; he gave gifts to his people." (When it says, "he ascended," what does it mean but that he had also descended into the lower parts of the earth? He who descended is the same one who ascended far above all the heavens, so that he might fill all things.) The gifts he gave were that some would be apostles, some prophets, some evangelists, some pastors and teachers, to equip the saints for the work of ministry, for building up the body of Christ, until all of us come to the unity of the faith and of the knowledge of the Son of God, to maturity, to the measure of the full stature of Christ. We must no longer be children, tossed to and fro and blown about by every wind of doctrine, by people's

trickery, by their craftiness in deceitful scheming. But speaking the truth in love, we must grow up in every way into him who is the head, into Christ, from whom the whole body, joined and knit together by every ligament with which it is equipped, as each part is working properly, promotes the body's growth in building itself up in love. (Eph. 4:1–6)

In light of our hypothesis—*God is continually calling to us. We can discern and follow God's leading*—what can we learn from these New Testament passages?

First, we see that not everyone who hears God calling will follow, at least not immediately. The rich young man seems to accept that Jesus speaks on God's behalf (or, at least, Mark accepts this), but when Jesus addresses him at the level of his unique spiritual struggle—his wealth—he is "shocked" and goes away "grieving." The shock and grief are because the truth of what Jesus says tugs at his heart, and he knows that he must either leave his possessions behind or forfeit eternal life. He clearly trusts that what Jesus says is true and now must make a decision, one that will change his life no matter which way he chooses. What Jesus has said demands a response. It meets the man right at the heart of his spiritual struggle.

Second, we can learn the importance of thinking about individual gifts, the unity of the body, and the relationship between them. The Ephesians passage highlights for the church the importance of each person living according to the gifts he or she has been given and the faith in Christ to which the church has been called. We can imagine that this letter is being written to people in a situation of *dis*unity, with the hope that they can work together for the loving unity that is truly of God. If we can jump over history and around puzzles about the Bible's relation to contemporary Christians, we can accept this demand to respect our particular gifts and the particular gifts of others and to understand all of them as aimed at the "work of ministry" and the growth of the body.

Third, taken together, these three passages from the New Testament encourage us to think about the context in which God's call is heard. The rich young man finds God addressing his basic struggle, not talking with him about irrelevant things. We who are relatively wealthy (a group that includes virtually everyone who is reading this book) would certainly not like to be told what to do with our possessions or our money. We are adept at rationalizing why we should not give away the many things we do not need (including cash) to those who are starving, homeless, or ill. Yet we can well imagine, given our wealth, that this is exactly the area to which God would have us pay attention. In Paul's case, he is a gifted man: educated, passionate, and theologically insightful. God recognizes the gifts but wants them used in a different way. The Ephesians passage speaks to our modern-day divisions in the church as well as those of Paul's time. It reminds us, in our context of disunity, to live first as Christians, in humility, patience, love, and seeking unity with our fellow Christians. We are to support others with different gifts than our own and to use our own gifts, along with theirs, for building up the body of Christ instead of tearing it apart.

Fourth, the grief the rich young man experienced at being told to give away all he has as well as the continuing disunity of even small clusters of Christians remind us that *it is sometimes easier to hear God's call than to follow it*. This challenge may be the most significant that these passages pose to our hypothesis. Perhaps God calls and perhaps we can discern God's call, but can we follow? Do we have the courage, humility, and love? As we move in the direction of some kind of summary statement about how to discern what God would have us do, we want to be sure that when we ask the question, we are ready to hear and live out the answer.

You may see other important points that we should learn from one or more of these biblical passages. You may also see additional ways in which our hypothesis is challenging or being challenged by this conversation partner. You will want to carry these into the final chapter with you, so jot them down here, while you are thinking of them. Then move to the following discussion of our second partner.

❖◦❖◦❖◦❖◦❖◦❖◦❖

Notes

❖◦❖◦❖◦❖◦❖◦❖◦❖

Historical Approaches to Christian Thinking and Living

A look through a book such as William Placher's *Callings: Twenty Centuries of Christian Wisdom on Vocation*[2] gives one a sense that the issues we are concerned with here are ones that have long occupied Christian thinkers. Placher makes it clear that the many voices that can be heard through the ages move from very early understandings where one was called simply to be Christian, to a millennium or so when the language of calling applied to the religious life, to the Reformation's focus on every legitimate work as a calling, to additional and diverse understandings that have arisen in the last few centuries. Of the many important voices one can hear in the tradition, one that stands out to me is the sixteenth-century Puritan William Perkins. In 1602, the year of his death, he published *A Treatise of the Vocations, or, Callings of men, with the sorts and kinds of them, and the right use thereof.*[3] Few contemporary Christians are likely to accept all of Perkins's answers, but more than any other single text, his essay thoroughly raises the issues relevant to vocation.

In a brief preface written to his "very good friend" Robert Taillor, Perkins argues that callings are one of God's ways of bringing good ("the honour and glorie of his name") out of the confusion created by the fall. Perkins says, "Few men rightly know how to live and goe on in their callings, so as they may please God" (750), so he sets out to instruct us. He writes his essay as a commentary on 1 Corinthians 7:20, which, in his King James Version of the Bible, reads, "Let every man abide in that calling, wherein hee was called."

Perkins defines vocation as *"a certaine kinde of life, ordained and imposed on man by God, for the common good"* (750; italics in original). We will look at what Perkins means by each piece of this definition, but you might pause and ponder it here. It is really quite a suggestive look at the idea with which we are wrestling. Who calls each one of us? God. To what? A particular way of life that God has chosen for us. Why? For the good of everyone. If we could fill in the details of each of those claims in a way that made sense to us theologically, we would be very far along the path of committing ourselves to a particular understanding of vocation. Of course, it is the details that matter when thinking about these issues. If you tried to sketch some of them in at this early point in our conversations, where would you come down? Who is God? To what does God call us? Why?

Declaring God to be the efficient cause (a technical expression in philosophy that means the author) of every calling, Perkins uses the metaphors of God as a military general and of humanity as a watch to fill in his claims:

> For looke as in the campe, the Generall appointeth to every man his place and standing; one place for the horse-man & another for the footman, and to every particular souldier likewise, his office and standing, in which hee is to abide against the enemie, and therein to live and die: even so it is in humane societies: God is the General, appointing to every man his particular calling, and as it were his standing: and in that calling he assignes unto him his particular office; in performance whereof he is to live & die. . . . Againe, in a clocke, made by the arte and handy-worke of man, there be many wheeles, and every one hath his severall motion, some turne this way, some that way, some goe softly, some apace: and they are all ordered by the motion of the watch. Behold here a notable resemblance of Gods speciall providence over mankinde, which is the watch of the great world, allotting to every man his motion and calling: and in that calling, his particular office and function. (750)

Excuse me, but did you actually read that paragraph? I do not mean to intrude on your reflections, but one of the things that can turn us off in historical materials is that we are not always accustomed to the language. But we can miss important material when we skim over such passages. In this case, we would miss a view of God and humanity that should certainly challenge us because of its importance for Christians through the ages. So, if you did not read the paragraph, go back and give it a shot. If you are still finding it difficult, then try putting it in contemporary English as you go: "Just as in a military camp, the General (or commanding officer) assigns to each person a particular duty . . . so God. . . ."

The quotation above raises the question of why God appoints us to different callings, though Perkins's mention of fighting against the enemy is suggestive in a Christian context. He goes on, however, to argue that God's purpose (the final cause) is the "common good" of humanity. He then appeals to the image of society as a body in which all the various parts work together for the good of the whole. He writes:

> The common good of men stands in this, not only that they live, but that they live well, in righteousnes and holinesse, & consequently, in true happinesse. And for the attainement hereunto, God hath ordained and disposed all callings, and in his providence, designed the persons to beare them. (751)

Perkins then notes that to make use of one's calling to benefit oneself alone is to abuse the calling.

You can see how all of the pieces fit together here. For Perkins, God wants each one of us to be happy. In order to be happy, we must be righteous and holy. So God has designed us and the world in such a way that we can be righteous and holy, and therefore happy, as long as we live according to our calling. When we all do this, society—like a body composed of pieces that are all working well and harmoniously—will be an orderly place filled with contented people. By staying true to our calling, we fulfill the main purpose of our lives, which is "to serve God in the serving of men in the workes of our callings" (757).

Perkins points out that some people are not living as they should. He quotes Jeremiah 48:10 ("*Cursed is hee that dooth the worke of the Lorde negligently*"; italics in original) to support his claim that two relevant and "damnable sinnes" are idleness and sloth (753). Later in the text, he writes against "rogues, beggars, vagabonds," "Monkes and Friars," (755) and people of leisure, none of whom "have a personal calling, in which they must performe some duties for the common good, according to the measure of the gifts that God hath bestowed on them" (756). On Perkins's view, all of these people are simply societal parasites, contributing nothing relative to what they take.

Perkins's essay is rich with convictions we could discuss, but here are just three more relevant to our pursuit. First, Perkins distinguishes between two kinds of vocation, the general and the particular: the first is the call from God to be a Christian; the second is "the execution of some particular office; arising of that distinction which God makes betweene man and man in every societie" (754). These two must be lived together; indeed, this is the key to a good life: "If thou wouldst leade a life unblameable both before God & man, thou must first of all bethink thy selfe, what is thy particular calling, and then proceede to practise duties of the morall law, and all other duties of Christianity, in that very calling" (757). Whatever we do as our calling, we must be moral people and faithful Christians if we are to live in right relationship with God and with our neighbors.

Second, Perkins has an answer for those of us who are trying to discern our calling. He says that "every man must examine himself of two things: first, touching his affection: secondly, touching his gifts." By "affection," Perkins has in mind both what we like and where we "desireth most of all to glorifie God" (758). When we choose our calling, we then have to discern the best way to live out our choice, which requires authorization from the appropriate human authorities.

Third, once in a given place, one can expect to face difficulties, but one should continue in that calling until some clear call tells one otherwise. Our callings set the parameters for our lives to a great extent: ". . . whatsoever any man enterprizeth or doth, ether in word or deede, he must doe it by vertue of his calling, and he must keepe himself within the compasse, limits, or precincts thereof" (751). Furthermore, "And as in a campe, no souldier can depart his standing, without the leave of the Generall; no more may any man leave his calling, except he receive liberty from God" (750), a liberty which becomes clear, in part, in the conscience of the individual. "Every man must judge that particular calling, in which God hath placed him, to be the best of all callings for him . . ." (756) until such time as it becomes clear that a change of calling is right.

Perkins addresses those who are trying to discern their calling, those who do not know or do not believe or do not care that they have a particular calling, those who are in a calling but are not acting in a Christian fashion, and those who are restless or dissatisfied in their calling. If you fall into any of those groups, you would find it profitable to track down and study carefully a complete version of Perkins's essay. For now, what do we hear in Perkins that is meaningful for the testing of our hypothesis, *God is continually calling to us. We can discern and follow God's leading*?

First, he challenges us to be clear about what we mean by "calling." If we limit our meaning to a momentary intervention to head us in a particular direction, we miss what he means. If we think of calling as a process of invitation, we also miss what he means. Perkins quite deliberately uses the language of "ordained and imposed" and the metaphor of the general on the battlefield. *God does not invite us to something but puts us where we belong.* God has designed it so that our gifts, other people's gifts, and society's needs fit together. If we are not living the vocation for which God has designed us, we are endangering the happiness of the whole society. The notion is balanced by some indications of human freedom, but if our view is that we must go looking all over the place to see what God wants, Perkins's view challenges us. What God wants is for us to live the moral, Christian, life right where we are.

Of course, we may not be happy in our calling, in the sense of having contented feelings about it, if we follow Perkins's path. You may have the sense already, and you will have a better sense if you read his entire work, that Perkins is not overly concerned with what we would today call happiness. His slight appeal to "affection" for our calling aside, it is clear that Perkins would not be interested in the "I'm bored (or otherwise dissatisfied) in my job; maybe I'll look for something else" approach to vocation. You are where you are meant to be, so do your job well and in a Christian spirit until there is some very clear sign that you should move. What such a sign would be, in Perkins's view, is difficult to know.

What do you think of Perkins's notion that we have both a general and a particular calling? These are sometimes referred to as primary and secondary callings, but the meaning is the same: we have a general calling that applies to all of us, and each one of us has a particular calling that is unique to her or him. The "we" of the general calling is, in Perkins's case, Christians, but we might also think of it as humanity. The list of particular callings, again for Perkins, includes king, magistrate, minister, master of a family, wife, apostle, physician, parent, parishioner, merchant, soldier, lawyer, carpenter, mason, shepherd, and prophet. These are examples, of course, not a complete list. The person or people (more than one person might be called to be a parent, after all) in each one of these callings must also live the Christian life. To the extent that this life has general norms or principles to it (such as "love your enemy"), each person, though in a different particular calling, will be living similarly insofar as being a Christian is concerned. If we agree with this approach when we say that God calls us, we will need to sort out not only what particular way of life God has in store for us, but also, in the current climate where defining what being a Christian means is a complex matter, what variety of Christian faith we will live out in that place.

A final point we might take from Perkins is to pay close attention to our gifts. Virtually everyone who talks about vocation talks about the uniqueness of our gifts: for Perkins, this is one of the ways God distinguishes between humans. This is a challenge to our hypothesis not because it is a controversial general idea, but because you have more than one gift. Virtually anything you do well qualifies as a gift in some sense: taking good photographs, arranging furniture in a room so that it fits its purpose, throwing a ball accurately, reading or writing, listening to friends in need, helping people to feel comfortable in conversations, baking, accounting, shopping for clothes for friends, giving people gifts that make them happy, being courageous or generous or merciful, reasoning well with unreasonable people, making others laugh, and swimming long distances are just a few examples.

Before you move on, take a few moments to list your gifts in the space provided. If you cannot think of any, ask each of five people who know you well to list one of your gifts. Your particular collection of gifts certainly do distinguish you from each other person in the world, but if what God is calling us to do is simply to use our gifts, we may find discerning what that means very difficult. This is another piece we will carry with us into the final chapter as we work to learn from, and teach, our conversation partners.

Notes

The Contemporary Christian World

Again, we remind ourselves of our shorthand hypothesis: *God is continually calling to us. We can discern and follow God's leading.* How might we best test this in the contemporary Christian world? We might seek feedback from friends who are Christians. We might peruse the shelves of our local bookstore looking for helpful literature. We might visit a variety of churches and talk to some of the people there. We might track down some Christian theologians and ask about how these issues are being understood in the academic theological world. No choice we make is going to give us even a representative sampling of the views of the more than two billion Christians who populate the earth, but each voice with which we consult is likely to add insight to our discussion.

I am convinced that we often learn more from those whose views differ from our own, so I decided to interview a local pastor with whom I differ on various theological issues. The Rev. Vickie Perkins (whom I will refer to as Vickie both since I actually know her and so that you do not confuse her with the William of the previous section, to whom I do not think she is related) is the pastor of Hanover United Methodist Church in Hanover, Indiana, not far from Hanover College, where I teach. She is a charismatic and caring person, an excellent musician, a beloved pastor, and a passionate Christian. Many people, of all ages and theological points of view, are attracted to the depth of self she puts into her sermons and her worship leadership, as well as her gifts for pastoral counseling (students seeking counsel commend her for asking them good questions instead of telling them what they should think). Vickie arrived at HUMC in 1996; under her leadership, this church and its community presence and outreach are growing significantly. I began our discussion by explaining to her the focus of this exploration and then asked her a series of questions.[4]

MD: Just to give the reader a sense of who they are talking to, Vickie, how would you place yourself theologically on the broad continuum of American Christians?

VP: I don't like labels because I think they distract us from what is really important in our faith, but I'm certainly on the conservative side of the spectrum. For the most part, I just like to say that I'm a sinner saved by grace.

MD: Fair enough. Would you describe for me your call to ministry?

VP: It has several parts. When I was ten and my father had just become a Christian, we received a call one day from a woman who wanted to end her life. She wanted to talk with my father, but he wasn't home. I remember the woman saying that she knew I was just a little girl, but she had no one to talk to. I remember telling her that God loved her. This was my first sense that God might have a purpose for me in ministry. But this original sense didn't survive my teen years. Over time and for many different reasons, I became more self-centered. I did ministry, but I did it as a performance and for the strokes I got from others. Over the years this felt like a burden, like I was in a stronghold or in Egypt, but I didn't see any way out. A series of events brought me to a horribly low point, where I stayed in some way or other for several years, but I emerged from that seeing God again more the way I saw Him as a child. I came to know Him, not just as a symbol, but personally. Today, when I ask myself if I could do any thing else but pastor and have joy in my work life, the answer is no. But now it's not for me, it's for Him.

MD: Can you say something about how God works in your life today?

VP: There are two things I know. First, God loves me unconditionally. I know that. Second, God walks with me in the cool of the garden. "With me" is how I describe my relationship with God. I know that God is with me. Not alongside me, not leading me, but with me, in my heart. Of course, that doesn't solve all of life's problems. For one thing, I have to choose every day to live according to what I know. We have the choice to choose for or against God, and it's a choice we have to make continually.

MD: Does God intervene in our lives?

VP: Yes, according to His eternal purpose. God's purpose is for us to love Him in Christ, to know Him and to live joyfully in that knowledge.

MD: What about all of the suffering you see around you?

VP: It's horrible and it changes anyone who sees it, but it was not part of God's purpose. We threw God's original blessing back in His face, and now we have another way to Him: through Christ. The suffering is not what God wants, but He allows it and will use it for his purpose.

MD: How do we know what God wants us to do, in particular situations or with our lives?

VP: I trust in His Word. The Scripture is foundational for me. Even if it does not contain precise instructions for every possible choice I have, it gives principles that show me the right direction. For instance, I may not find an answer to the question of whether to buy a certain item, but I do learn in the Word what good stewardship is and how to view possessions. As far as what we should do with our lives, God has an answer there, too. We look to the gifts we have been given, to the Word, and to what brings us true joy. Little by little, paying attention to these things will show us where we should go.

MD: Does God ever speak to you?

VP: Yes, but not in an audible voice. It is a voice that is distinguishable from my own, though. One time when I was at the very bottom of my journey, in the deepest valley, with nothing to turn to, I fell on the floor under the cross in our sanctuary and simply said, "Here I am." I gave myself fully to God in that moment in a way I had never done before. And I heard God, in a voice I had never heard, say, "Get up." Again, not an audible voice, but a voice in my Spirit.

MD: How do you know when it is God's voice?

VP: Because it is never something that I could have conceived. I once saw a woman walking barefoot on a snowy day. I am not by nature a very generous person, but I heard so clearly God saying, "Give her your shoes." So I did. It's a scary thing to follow what God says and sometimes I just can't quite do it, but when I can there is always a blessing that follows.

MD: What would you say to someone who said you are just deluded about all of this and that there is no God?

VP: For me, nothing makes sense without Him. In the end, you cannot disprove what has happened to me. And I would not be here were it not for Him.

In Vickie's view, God is a being who speaks to our hearts. God is with us always and loves us unconditionally. God does not necessarily protect us from harm but is within us as guide and comforter. God intervenes, not arbitrarily, though it might appear that way from our point of view, but according to God's purpose and plan. We are free to choose for God or against God; when we choose for God, God's presence becomes more and more clear.

Vickie refers to Scripture as her "foundation," and it is the primary way God calls to us. The level of authority she grants to Scripture means that it requires some kind of response from her. This is not a simplistic relationship, not a straightforward matter of reading and then acting, but a very complex one in which she works diligently and passionately to discern God's Word to her. As Vickie experienced as a young child, God can also call us through events. God called her again through her emotional and spiritual struggles, not giving them to her but allowing her to have them so that she would recognize that she needed to live differently. Were we to generalize this, perhaps we could say that certain events trigger the recognition that God is calling someone in a certain direction. God also calls, in Vickie's view, through something like direct speech. It is not that God speaks aloud to us or that we hear God with our ears, but that something like a voice resonates in our hearts, telling us what to do. She appeals to one of the traditional guidelines for determining whether the voice one "hears" is God's or one's own: if you are told to do some good thing you never would have thought of doing on your own, it is more likely to be God's voice than yours. (This is, of course, a potentially dangerous guideline and one that should not be trusted if what we think we are told to do would cause any harm to anyone.)

Vickie's experiences and understandings would seem to affirm significant parts of our shorthand hypothesis: *God is continually calling to us. We can discern and follow God's leading.* At the same time, she does not have the doubts about the nature of God that are suggested in our longer version. We have raised questions about whether God is a being and whether God intervenes; these are not Vickie's questions.

An additional part of Vickie's view that is worth considering is her sense that she can sometimes hear God's call but is not always willing to follow. Where do you stand on this? Have you ever thought you knew what God wanted, or even known almost for sure what God wanted of you, but just could not bring yourself to do it? For Vickie, one impact of this decision is that it may be more difficult to hear God speak the next time (whether by God's choice or on account of your own). Has that been your experience? It is a traditional teaching in Christian spirituality that not following God's Word means God's speaking will be less evident in the future. Vickie also says that not responding to what she knows is God brings with it a deep sense of grief, just as we saw in the rich young man of the Mark story. Do you agree? Our later discussions about discernment must take issues such as these into account, so we should hold onto them as we move ahead.

Finally, it is worth mentioning that our courage will be challenged if we adopt the view Vickie is trying to live. Imagine driving along in the winter and feeling as though you should give your shoes to someone walking along the side of the road. Would you stop and do it? Would it matter what the person looked like? Just as many have held the view that not paying attention to God on one occasion may make it more difficult to listen the next time, so many have said that God speaks more often once we do listen. Imagine how more and more frequent encounters with and instructions from God would change your life.

Christian Religious Experiences

Listening to and learning from our own experiences and the experiences of our fellow Christians is a necessary guide for living well in the world. We learn what it means to be a Christian when we watch others do it; we learn how to name who we are and for what purpose we are here only as we hear the stories told by others; we understand our own experiences of faith and lack of faith as others share their experiences and become our guides. Do you have people in your life who are truly Christian mentors for you? If so, you know how important they can be to your spiritual growth. If not, do not be afraid to talk to people whose Christian living you admire as you seek models for your life.

As important as religious experiences can be, they are most valuable when they are critically assessed. In a culture that is obsessed with the inner world and with even the most insignificant experiences, we learn the most from experiences, whether our own or someone else's, when we think carefully about them. Unexamined experiences are rather like theories without heart: they frequently lead us to places where we do not really want to be.

The reading list for this chapter includes some books that contain experiences, fictional or factual, that might be relevant to your faith and theological journey. Instead of discussing one of those here, however, I am going to share something an old friend recently told me. I had not talked with Carol in at least twenty-five years when I received an e-mail from her a few months ago. After a few e-mail exchanges and on a whirlwind tour to see friends and family before heading out of the country for a while, she stopped by to visit for a couple of days. As we talked, she shared some recent experiences that she understands as God calling her to a new place in life. After she left and I continued to ponder what God might have in store for her, I decided to ask her to write her experience so that I might use it here.[5]

This is what she wrote:

When my friend Pam, a wife and the mother of three young children, shares the story of how she decided to enter seminary, she always concludes with some variation on what has become her favorite phrase: "I can't not." Her story is one of a tug-of-war struggle and profound doubt, but she remains convicted—yesterday she wrote to me, "I am driven beyond logic to do whatever it is that I am doing here."

Pam heard God calling, and against all logic, she responded "yes."

I've had the privilege of enduring a similar experience recently, and like Pam, I have chosen to believe that it was (and indeed still is) God presenting me with a challenge to step out of my box. I say, "enduring," because it took me a long time to build my sturdy and familiar cube—I could never *intentionally* abandon it! So how did I end up not only outside, but buckled into this roller coaster–like process of "being called"? Pam likens it to being "driven"; I think of it as being "pulled" or even "lured." Either way, it's been my experience that He doesn't force you to climb in, but does demand a response to His offer of a ride. Logic rarely plays into the decision, and I've found the destination (if there even is one) is never revealed. But what an awe-full revelation that you're indeed being invited to come along! And when the call seems so loud and clear, as the one I've received recently seems to be, how could I not accept? Following is a description of the major events leading up to my "yes."

As an Elder in the Presbyterian Church (USA), I have watched people grow in their faith, and being privy to this process is always a great blessing. I have myself grown, mainly through the love and patience of a wonderful mentor and friend, my Associate Pastor Nancy. But the growing process has an ebb and flow to it, and a few months ago, feeling the flow stagnate and my leadership effectiveness burn out, I took a one-week period of "personal exile." I began trying to formulate an answer to the question asked by most (if not all) mid-lifers: "What do I want to do with the rest of my life?" At about the same time, I decided to look up an old friend with whom I used to love to ponder questions like this. . . . We began corresponding via e-mail, and in the process of catching up on decades past, I discovered (or was led to discover?) a possible answer to my life-question, buried in a message I'd written to him:

[As Elder for Adult Nurture,] I've taught Bible studies and lead a couple women's retreats, and just love it. This work over the past 5 years has grown in me a deep-seated passion (rooted in my own faith story) to discover how church leaders can (help God) "Equip the Saints," how people grow spiritually, how to help them discern their vocation in the Church. . . .

No one will convince me that the timing of my reunion with Mike was coincidental. In conversing with my long-lost friend, I had actually articulated (for the first time to anyone) my intense desire to be involved in the spiritual growth process of others, just as others had been for me. In fact, the mere existence of this passion took me by surprise.

I heard several other rumblings during my exile week. (Let me add that I seem to hear best during a quiet time apart, or during a faith crisis experience of emptiness.)

Early on that week, I had a casual discussion with Nancy about her desire to start a Center for Spiritual Direction at our church. I'd had no exposure to this type of ministry before then. We talked about each "butterfly" we had known over the years—someone whose faith had emerged from the "chrysalis" to become beautiful, more mature, and able to fly. She lent me a book by Margaret Guenther called *Holy Listening*, and invited me to mark it up as I wished. I took it, thinking I probably wouldn't be interested enough to do much more than skim it, let alone mark it up. Well, I not only marked it up, I devoured it. I learned that there is a name for the spiritual companionship I'd experienced with Nancy and others; there is a ministry that addresses my newly found passion—it's called being a Spiritual Director, engaging in the ministry of Spiritual Direction. I recognized myself as a Directee, having been on the receiving end of this special relationship.

Some of the aspects of the Director's role also resonated with me. My perpetual intrigue with how to "listen well to God" was addressed. The element of teaching in this ministry excited me. My fear of risk-taking was allayed as I began to understand that the Holy Spirit is the *true* Director—and I get to be a part of His process. So many other things I read took my breath away. Perhaps most striking (and this paradox always seems to play out for me when it appears that God's involved) were the many qualities of Spiritual Directors that I would *never* use to describe myself. Guenther suggests that Directors are willing to be open, gladly sharing their space; must let themselves be touched; abandon their defenses; have no fear of intimacy with another person; are not there to "fix" the other; are attentive and merciful. (My "Mercy" score on Spiritual Gifts Inventories could not be lower.) *Come on, who am I kidding?* For a week after finishing this casually lent out book, and alone in my house, I paced, I cried, I shook my head and laughed, I panicked, I hardly ate, I hardly slept. The supernaturalness of the experience, to my mind, was unmistakable. I could not ignore what was happening, and urgently needed to think about what I thought I was hearing, and what to respond.

I emerged at the end of my week "in the wilderness" to attend church. My beloved Senior Pastor spoke of "Easter Amnesia"—our tendency to forget the gloriousness of the Resurrection, thereby missing the opportunity for God's transforming work. When he said the "fear of risk" is a symptom of this condition, my heart leapt and sank at the same time. *Please stop calling and give me a minute to digest all of this, Lord—*

The next day, I met up with my husband and daughter in Fort Lauderdale, where they had been doing some dad-daughter vacationing. My in-laws were there as well. My mind was reeling, and I was exhausted. I told my story of discovery, and I received the whole-hearted and most significant affirmations from my family members.

The "butterfly" conversation with Nancy had stayed with me. A beautiful sailboat glided by the house that afternoon. It was named "Chrysalis." And believe it or not, a monarch butterfly followed behind it. And still He persisted—when I asked my daughter what she was reading that same afternoon, she replied "A book for school—*Madame Butterfly*." *Okay, Okay, Hound of Heaven—I give up! Please, just let me rest. I promise to get back to You.*

In the days that followed, I shared my experience with trusted friends, all of whom commented that "this is a no-brainer." (Easy for them to say.) My brother (another of my spiritual mentors) came for a rare visit during this time, and listened patiently to my story and the associated fears and excuses as to why I couldn't possibly do this. After all, it would involve stepping down early from my position as Elder, going back to school, writing papers (!), and perhaps even going back to full-time work if I were to get involved with the new Center at church. He ran upstairs to get his Bible. He was reading *The Message*[6] cover-to-cover, and through watery eyes he read that day's passage to me:

> Luke 9:57–62: On the road someone asked if he could go along. "I'll go with you, wherever," he said. Jesus was curt: "Are you ready to rough it? We're not staying in the best inns, you know." Jesus said to another, "Follow me." He said, "Certainly, but first excuse me for a couple of days, please. I have to make arrangements for my father's funeral." Jesus refused. "First things first. Your business is life, not death. And life is urgent: Announce God's kingdom!" Then another said, "I'm ready to follow you, Master, but first excuse me while I get things straightened out at home." Jesus said, "No procrastination. No backward looks. You can't put God's kingdom off till tomorrow. Seize the day."

Enough. I answered "yes." I couldn't not. That's just the way it seems to work when God calls.

And so the real ride begins! I have been accepted into a year-long ministry program at Oxford University, and I will eventually specialize in Spiritual Direction. My pastors are excited at the prospect of developing The Chrysalis Center for Spiritual Direction. I am anxious and exhilarated, distracted yet driven. And I anticipate many more ups and downs as this journey continues. But isn't that what a roller coaster ride is all about?

What do you think about that story? I think we can learn a lot from it. Notice the many pieces to Carol's process here: initial discontentment with who/where she is; time away in a week of exile; contact with people who, even if unconsciously, suggest to her another direction; reading; events that nag and pull, seemingly in an effort to get her to pay attention; fear, resistance, panic, tears; discussions with family and trusted friends; an encounter with the Bible; an ongoing conversation with God; acceptance of the path and setting out on a new adventure. Not everyone will go through the same process, of course. It is not a process that we can or should try to universalize or codify, but many of its pieces are frequently part of what Christians describe as being called by God.

What in this story have we seen in earlier conversations and what is new to this one? We have certainly watched people interpreting various experiences of "calling" as being from God. What is reinforced in Carol's experience is God's persistence. Remember Samuel being called three times by God before he understood what was happening? Remember Vickie being called early in her life, but living her call in the wrong way until God called again through her distress? In Carol's experience, she hears God calling and is reluctant to respond affirmatively until she is very clear that it is God doing the calling and not just a midlife crisis of her own making. She sees event after event, a dozen of them by my count, as God's activity in her life until she finally says "yes."

In further conversation with me, Carol noted the depth of contentment that seems to underlie this process, or at least its aftermath, a sense that this is what she is supposed to be doing, even if she doesn't know why or where she will end up. It's not that she supposes everything is going to be easy, but that the road is the right one and God is the one with ultimate control. This inner contentment, some would call it joy, may be an additional sign that we are on the road on which God wants us to be.

In discussing the essay by William Perkins, we saw the distinction between general and particular callings. The first is the call to be a Christian. The second is the call to the unique way of life that expresses a person's gifts and desires. Both are done in the service of others. Carol's story reinforces the idea of particular calling. Her gifts of intelligence and compassion, her supportive friends and family, and her desire to accompany others on their journeys with God, come together in a unique way to point her in one particular direction. That direction may change, of course, as she moves forward, but that would be consistent with being in the middle of a discernment process. As with Abram, she has been told to "Go," or perhaps called to follow. To where and for what purpose is not yet clear.

Something else we see repeated in Carol's experience is the sense that God is calling her to something she would not have identified for herself. We saw this in Vickie's claim that when God speaks to her it is usually to tell her to do something not obviously consistent with her personality. Likewise with Carol, who sees herself being called out of her comfortable world into a life that demands gifts, such as mercy, that she does not believe she has. We might also think back on the stories of Moses and Jeremiah here; if you read more of those stories than I quoted, you know that in both of these cases we have people who doubted their gifts for doing what God asked of them. What we typically hear in these cases is that God makes possible what people believed was impossible.

You should be sorting through how some of these issues have played out in your own life. Are there places where you heard God but resisted doing what God asked? Do you accept the view that God often calls us to expand our horizons and do something we did not think we could do? When you are making a crucial decision, do you consult friends and family, listen to the Scripture, talk to a pastor, take time away, express your emotions, watch for synchronicities, and read meaningful books? Which of these do you find most and least helpful? Are there additional resources you draw on in your decision making? As you reflect on these things, you move closer and closer to constructing your view of God and God's calling to you.

Non-Christian Knowledge and Ways of Knowing

Accepting the idea that God calls us to certain ways of life is a way to give meaning and purpose to what we do. You may view your life as a parent, grandparent, son or daughter, arborist, cashier, office manager, teacher, business executive, loan officer, auto mechanic, ship captain, or triathlete quite differently if you believe it is the life God calls you to live than if you believe otherwise. For instance, you will understand your roles in life through an entirely different set of symbols (the kingdom of God, perhaps, or sin and redemption) if you view them as relevant to God in some way. If God authorizes or appoints us to do what we do or to be who we are, we have the strongest possible reasons to pursue what we see as our vocation.

Not everyone finds their meaning or purpose through a relationship with God, however, and we Christians must consider their challenges to us. Consider, first, something Michael Novak says in his book *Business As a Calling: Work and the Examined Life*. Novak's book is a multilayered one, speaking about the moral heart of business to people who find meaning in many different places. Novak rightly notes that many of "America's well-educated elites" do not think about vocation or anything else in religious terms.

> Though they are likely to speak of knowing themselves, finding their own identity, seeking their own fulfillment, even "doing their own thing," what they are doing is very like responding to a calling. . . . Within limits, all of us are talking about pretty much the same thing. We are probably flexible enough to try on each other's language and to translate from one to the other as needed.[7]

Whether you take the "limits" Novak mentions to be many or few, his claim should inspire you to think about a crucial question: "if the issue of what I am to do with my life can be equally well explored outside of the very difficult theological issues we have been contemplating, why not just make life easier for myself and eliminate all this talk about God?" We could translate our hypothesis into, "Some ways of life will be more fulfilling to me than others. There are ways to discover what these are." Before we decide what we need to retain from this partner as we continue evaluating our hypothesis, we must consider an even more direct challenge to the entire enterprise in which we are engaged.

Consider these words from a philosophy major at Hanover, Jay Hamman:

> People cling to ideas such as God, Truth, Justice, and Vocation in order to bring meaning to a meaningless existence. Human beings need assumptions, anchors, to make their way through life. Without these anchors humans drift into nihilistic skepticism, lying in bed waiting for the release that death could possibly bring.[8]

The challenge here is not that there might be more than one valid way of discussing the idea of whether we are called, but that there are, in a sense, *no* valid ways. Whatever language we might use, however helpful it is in anchoring us to the world, merely covers up the meaninglessness of existence. It would be consistent with the tiny piece of Michael Novak's view that we have cited to say that there are several approximately equal ways of talking about our meaningful existence. In Jay Hamman's view, the ways of talking may be equal, but what they are equally good at is covering up the fact that life means nothing.

You will need to reflect on both of these voices as you continue to assess either our common hypothesis on vocation or the one you developed earlier on your own. Novak's words challenge our hypotheses because they make us stop and think why we insist on being Christians in the first place. They also make us wonder whether our Christian commitments are the best ones through which to discover our callings. Perhaps God is calling you, but if you can figure out to what you are called without having to sort through issues such as whether God intervenes in our lives, would that not be a good thing?

Hamman's views, at least when he wrote those words, challenge us to consider whether we are just kidding ourselves. Perhaps when it comes right down to it, there is no such thing as a calling, no such thing as a God who wants me to fulfill some particular role, and no need for anything like a process of discernment that would help me to discover my calling or role. Instead, perhaps there is simply personal choice. I choose to live the way I choose to live; if I am happy or unhappy, that has to do with my lot in life and the choices I have made, not whether I am doing what God wants me to do. Just as many people in our contemporary world are nonreligious, so are many convinced that personal preference is the key to the good life. Some people in both categories also believe that life in and of itself has no meaning. If you are confused and overwhelmed with thinking about this, do not worry; you will have a way to respond to these challenges before you finish the final chapter.

Non-Christian Religious Traditions

Do you know anyone from a different faith tradition than your own? I do not mean another branch of Christianity, but another of the world's major faith traditions—such as Islam, Judaism, Hinduism, Taoism, Confucianism, and Buddhism. In more ways than ever before, we American Christians are being challenged to expand our religious awareness by the growing presence of persons of other faith traditions in our midst. The reading list for this chapter suggests some places to start reflecting both upon these traditions and the importance to Christians of being in meaningful dialogue with them. If you want to begin immediately, you might read Diana Eck's book, *A New Religious America*.[9] It and its predecessor, *Encountering God*, invite us to ponder what reality is all about, to stretch our horizons of understanding, to expand our circle of care. If you know people from a different major faith tradition, you might begin to talk with them about the way they see life and faith. Although I know that some Christians, including perhaps you, will disagree with me, I am convinced that other faith traditions are a crucial conversation partner for Christians concerned with the shape and fate of the world. Whatever your convictions on this issue, I invite you to read this section with the same careful attention you have given to the previous sections. If you can accept that other traditions are our final conversation partner, what can we learn from them? If you do not accept this, how will you support your view?

So, we begin. Numerous voices can be heard within each world religion. Like Christianity, each one represents multiple subtraditions, and each subtradition represents multiple clusters of people in conversation, sometimes agreeing and sometimes disagreeing. Frankly, I am not an expert on any of these religions, traditions, or voices. As I discuss Buddhism, therefore, you should ponder several things: Is what I say more reflective of academic Buddhism, as, for instance, some Christian discussions of the Trinity might be, or am I in touch with the Buddhist on the street? Am I emphasizing what is most important in the tradition, or have I missed its point? Am I writing with sufficient distance from my own Christian views, or am I seeing Buddhism through eyes that corrupt its actual meaning? However many books I may have read through the years to try to understand Buddhism, you should see my conclusions and suggestions as tentative ones.

As the story goes, in the sixth century BCE, a royal couple in the Himalayas gave birth to a child named Siddhartha Gautama. Miracles and mysteries surrounded his conception and birth. When she became pregnant, his mother dreamed that a sacred white elephant entered her side. His father was told in a prophecy that his son would be either a great secular leader or a great sacred leader. When Gautama was born, he took several steps and announced that he was entering his final life, his final reincarnation.

Gautama grew up shielded from suffering. Whenever he left the palace, for instance, his father had the streets cleared of anyone who might be sick or poor. The gods conspired, however, and the young prince encountered what are called the Four Passing Sights: he saw an elderly person, a sick person, a corpse, and a holy man. Discovering that the first three represented parts of every person's life, but also seeing that there are people who try to find their way out of these apparent inevitabilities, Gautama kissed his wife and child good-bye one night and left the palace behind.

Gautama first joined with a variety of holy men, countering the extreme wealth of his past with extreme asceticism. He is said to have eaten only a few grains of rice a day and to have been able to touch his spine by pushing on his stomach. One day he passed out from lack of food, which encouraged him to leave his asceticism behind and seek truth in another way. At the age of thirty-five, while meditating under a pipal tree and surviving attacks by Mara the Tempter, he reached Enlightenment, becoming the Buddha, the Enlightened One. For forty-five years the Buddha taught, dying at the age of eighty. His final words urged his disciples to find their own way to the truth, to be a lamp unto themselves.

Key elements of the Buddha's teaching and of contemporary Buddhist life and practice include the Three Refuges, the Four Noble Truths, and the Noble Eightfold Path. The first, taking refuge in the Buddha, the Dharma, and the Sangha, is what it takes to become a Buddhist: to see the Buddha as one's guide, to follow the teachings of the Buddha, and to accept the support of the community of believers. The Four Truths give the context within which we all live and point us to the way out: all life is suffering, suffering is caused by desire, desire can be stopped, desire is stopped by living the Eightfold Path. This path is made up of right beliefs, right intentions, right speech, right action, right livelihood, right effort, right mindfulness, and right concentration. Right livelihood is the idea that overlaps most immediately with our exploration of vocation.

Perhaps because right action and right speech cover many of the possibilities, right livelihood often receives less attention than those in the writings on Buddhism that I have seen. There are, however, three aspects of right livelihood about which you should know. The first is the limitations the Buddha placed on appropriate ways to make a living. The second is the role of morality in guiding the work life one has, so that whatever one is doing one needs to do in a certain way (you can see here similarities with Perkins's general and particular callings). The third is the mindfulness that is appropriate to finding one's right livelihood. Can you see how these will fit with things we have already discussed?

First, the Buddha said that people should not make their living by doing anything that harmed or supported the harming of human beings or animals. One should not, for instance, be a butcher, a seller of weapons, or a seller of alcohol. Second, these restrictions appear to be just examples of the broader moral requirements of the Eightfold Path, requirements that are fundamental to further development on the path to Enlightenment. Moral behavior, principally compassion and not harming others in various specified ways, is required for the clarity of mind on which achieving Enlightenment depends. Third, mindfulness is a Buddhist tool for overcoming the temptations of the ego. It can be used not only for doing our current work well (without the desire to make excessive money, for instance) but also for discerning our right work and when to move from one workplace to another (by helping us to discern all aspects of the current situation clearly). Mindfulness is about paying attention and being present in the moment.

Translate these three points into language with which you are most familiar and decide what you think about them. Are there some ways of life, some roles or practices, to which God would not call us? Is this because some roles and practices violate moral teachings by which God wants us to live? How does paying attention in the moment help me to decide to what God is or is not calling me? Thinking back on William Perkins for a moment, we might also find a fourth question implicit in my very brief description of mindfulness: Do some of my desires, a characteristic Perkins noted as possibly pointing us toward our vocation, actually get in the way of discerning our vocation? Might a choice to be a physician, for instance, come from a desire to be respected in a society that venerates physicians rather than from a desire to help others? In Buddhism, at least, the former would be more likely to lead us astray than the latter.

These questions are more loosely related to their Buddhist counterparts than the word "translate" suggests, for Buddhists have no God. There is no sacred being who has created the world and rules over it, no omnipotent or otherwise perfect being to call us to a particular way of life. This does not mean there is no reality against which our actions can be measured, however. As some of Michael Novak's "well-educated elites" might measure the rightness or wrongness of actions or ways of life against the preferences (or some other characteristic) of the self, so the Buddhist might measure these against the steps along the path to the goal of nirvana, the ultimate state of peace. Putting it more simply than it probably should be put, actions that are consistent with the path to Enlightenment are right; those that are inconsistent are wrong.

It is almost impossible for the contemporary Christian in America not to harm others. Some of this is obvious to us, if we pause to think about it for a moment. We know that we can be rude to people, insult them, ignore them, and exclude them. Some of the harm we do is a bit less direct or immediate, but news reports make us aware of it regularly. We pollute the environment, refuse to stand up for what is right when this would come at a cost, hoard our money, and feed our children junk. Some of the harm we do is almost completely unintentional and unknown, but we recognize it when it is pointed out. We invest in companies (or in companies that do business with companies) that pollute excessively. We accept our own numbness when faced with others who have desperate needs. We consume without regard to the consequences for future generations. To use characteristically Christian language, we are sinners and are immersed in the world's fallenness.

What does this mean for thinking about vocation? It reminds us that how we live in our vocation is perhaps as important as what our vocation is—an insight we have seen before in Perkins. It also reminds us that, while assessments of the moral implications of various vocations are very important, it may be impossible to find a way of life that does not connect us in any way to the harm of others. It also leads us to think about how we would respond to someone who could only find a job building weapons or making cigarettes and who, otherwise, could not feed his or her family. Should we accept the view that this is wrong? Or, ask yourself, "Is it consistent with your view of God that someone be called to a job that includes executing convicted murderers, testing potentially deadly drugs on animals, or making trade agreements with countries that have records of serious human rights violations?" Is a way of life only a true vocation if it includes no possibility of being associated with harming another human being?

These kinds of questions remind us of the importance of mindfulness in our lives. I believe I am not alone in so often having my attention focused on the past or the future that being present to the current moment can be difficult. Is that your experience of life? As I ponder the Buddhist focus on paying attention to the moment, I am reminded of at least two things. I am reminded that any vocation is lived moment by moment, so that I am not answering God's call faithfully if I simply say, "Okay, I'll be a teacher," without listening in the moment to what it means to teach as God wants me to teach. And I am reminded that discerning whether something is or is not my intended way of life includes careful attention to the signs, signs that we discuss in the final chapter. These are two of the things we should take with us as we assess our hypothesis: *God is continually calling to us. We can discern and follow God's leading.*

Congratulations

This is a good place to pause and congratulate yourself on making it through some complex material. If you have done the hard work of paying attention, assessing what I have been saying, justifying both your criticisms and your agreements, and developing your own theological point of view, you deserve applause. Both the breadth and the depth of material you have covered to this point have been significant. If you are like many people I know and have trouble celebrating your own accomplishments, please accept congratulations from me.

One of my friends keeps asking me when I am going to give the answers to all of these great questions, especially the one about how we know what God is calling us to do. She is never happy when I tell her that theologians do not have answers, only questions. I am partly kidding about that, but you will find that the hard work you have been doing as you have read along is going to pay off with more answers than anything I might have to tell you. My voice is at best a guide as you discern what is happening in your own heart and mind.

In a moment, you will enter the final chapter of this book. If there is anything we have done in the current chapter or the previous ones that you either do not understand or think is just plain wrong, you should review that now. If you do not understand it, do your best to make sense of it by considering how it fits in with the rest of the material. If you disagree with something you have read, then articulate as carefully as possible why you disagree and how you would change what I have said in order to make it right. That will then show you how to modify the arguments and claims of the final chapter so that they make sense to you.

Since not all of the "answers" appear at once in the next chapter, you might like to know what is going to happen there. First, we are going to remind ourselves quickly about what theology and faith are. Second, we are going to put together everything we have learned from our conversations with our partners and see whether or not our hypothesis has held up, in both its long and its short forms. The critical and ethical guidelines that were introduced in chapter 3 will help us to do this. Third, you will see that there is, indeed, a meaningful sense in which God calls us and that it is possible, even if sometimes difficult, to discern that call. You will be given an approach to hearing God's call to you, along with some recommendations for how to think about your general and particular callings. In part, your discernment will depend upon your continuing commitment to answer the question "Who is God?" and your reflections upon the nature of love. Fourth, I address the large concerns raised by some of our partners about whether it makes any sense to hold onto Christian convictions about God. Finally, I say just a word or two about how any of this might apply in the social contexts in which we live our lives: what would a community or institution look like if it were truly to encourage the search for vocation? When you have satisfied yourself that you have sufficiently mastered what has come before, I invite you to consider the "answers" in chapter 7.

Questions for Reflection

1. What is your approach to reading the Bible?
2. What did you agree with and disagree with in what Perkins said? Do you like his metaphor of God as a general? Why or why not? What do you see as the common good?
3. What do you think your gifts say about your vocation?
4. Does Vickie Perkins, the United Methodist minister, describe a theological view that matches your own? What would you have wanted to ask her, and what do you think she would have said?

5. Have you "endured" any experiences like my friend Carol's? Was your process similar? If it was in some ways different, what can we learn from those differences?

6. Where do you see joy and contentment in your life? What do you think would make you more joyful or content?

7. Do you think we lose anything if we translate from theological to secular language? Do we lose anything that matters for the exploration of vocation?

8. What have you learned from other faith traditions? How do you think Christians should respond to other traditions? Do you agree with my view? Why or why not?

7

God, Love, and Vocation

The most basic of our goals in the previous chapter was to determine whether our hypothesis could legitimately be seen as part of the conversations that we Christians have in our search for convictions on which to base our lives. Although it is not likely that we will find a way to decide exactly which hypotheses fit and which ones do not fit, recognizing that we have a certain common understanding about some of the limits is important. Consider the hypothesis "God is a cat." That notion would just not fit in the Christian conversation. Christians could certainly discuss the issue, but, given the nature of Christianity, it would not make sense for any of us to hold this as a basic conviction.

Our hypothesis—*God is continually calling to us. We can discern and follow God's leading*—does, however, fit within the broad parameters of Christian conversations. We would typically not tell someone who made this claim that he or she must be talking about some other God or some other human beings. It clearly makes sense for a Christian to accept and live by this conviction. It is important to take the small step of acknowledging that. We now know that we can legitimately move forward with our theological work.

On our way to establishing a final conviction on vocation on which we can, in concert with other tested convictions, base our lives as

147

Christians, we must take a few final steps. First, we must review what we have learned from our partners about the content of our particular conviction. This will include combining the many dimensions of our conversations with the partners into a small number of categories or questions. Second, once we have processed the conversations as best we can, we need to state and briefly examine our final conviction. Third, we must be sure our final conviction can satisfy the conditions for a well-formed theological conviction. With the necessary theological work behind us to answer the question of whether God is calling, each of us will be able to put that work together with some discernment guidelines to answer the question of what God is calling us to do. You should not get your heart set on having an answer jump magically from the page; instead, you will have the tools you need to faithfully make some decisions.

Learning from Our Partners

Gathering together the various insights offered by the partners, I have listed below the things we learned from them that merit consideration as we move forward. These claims are only possibilities: without supporting arguments, we might not be able to accept any of them without revision or analysis. They are significant portions of what our partners have said that relate, directly or indirectly, to vocation, but we have not discussed important issues such as how they should be interpreted or valued, or how they should be balanced with one another. Christians address these issues in many different ways.

From the Bible, we learned that:

1. God seems to pop into certain lives at unpredictable moments and call people to new ways of being.
2. Education in hearing God might be important for discernment.
3. It could be that God enables us to do what God calls us to do.
4. God might or might not call continually as opposed to periodically.
5. God might or might not call us in the same way God called biblical figures.
6. God might or might not have human characteristics.

7. God may, in some cases, speak to our unique spiritual struggle.
8. Our individual gifts might be important and intended by God to be used in building up the wider community (or body of Christ).
9. It could be that our primary calling is to live as Christians.
10. Following God's call might not always be easy.

From historical approaches, we saw that:

1. It may be the case that God has put us right where God wants us.
2. Whether or not we feel happy may not be a sure guide to determining whether we are in the right place.
3. We might have both general (love your neighbor) and particular (be a teacher) callings.
4. One way to distinguish us from one another may be by our gifts.
5. We may well have more gifts than we can use in a single calling.

From contemporary Christians, we heard that:

1. It could be that God calls in many different ways, including through Scripture, in daily events, and by direct command.
2. It might be that one way to discern whether God is calling is to consider whether we would have thought of a particular action on our own.
3. We may not always have the personal resources to follow God's call.
4. There may be consequences, such as a feeling of grief, to ignoring a command from God.

From Christian religious experiences, we learned that:

1. There may be numerous parts to any given discernment process, including discontentment, time away, discussion with others, synchronistic events, varied emotions, biblical encounters, and prayer.
2. It could be that God will repeat a call over and over if we do not initially respond.
3. An indicator of a calling found and lived may be an underlying sense of contentment.

4. One indication of God's call may be that we are called to something we would not have thought of on our own.
5. It could be that God makes possible what seems impossible.

From non-Christian points of view, we are challenged that:

1. It could be that Christian language adds little to discussions of vocation.
2. It could be that there is no God and no vocation, but that these are simply ways of making a meaningless world meaningful.

From non-Christian religions, we see that:

1. It could be that some of our personal desires get in the way of discerning our vocation.
2. How we live in our place of calling may well be as important as where that place is.
3. Finding a calling in life may not eliminate the importance of listening to God in the moment.

How can we pull all of these thoughts and possibilities together into something coherent with which we can work? If you begin to rearrange them by topic, you will find that they divide pretty quickly into four sets of issues: the nature of God, what it means to say that God is calling us, how we should respond to God's call, and how we can discern what God would have us do. In question form, then, we have: Who is God? What is God doing? (Or what does it mean to say God is "calling"?) What does God want me to do? How do I know?[1]

If we ask our partners collectively to say *who God is*, we will find that most of them say that God is personlike, has broad plans that we cannot always understand, and intervenes in the world to further these plans by demanding action on our part. They also say that God knows us intimately and will enable us to do what God demands that we do if we will just trust and follow God's leading. If we ask *what God is doing*, the partners describe God as doing something closer to "demanding" than "inviting," the word I used previously. Demands do not rule out choices on our part, but they are not like invitations that arrive in the mail and simply disappear if we do not respond. As far as our partners are concerned, God's demands are repeated, and there can be negative consequences if we do not respond positively.

What does God want me to do? Our partners' responses fall into four categories. First, God may or may not call us to be Christians as opposed to having some other religious faith orientation or none at all. Second, there are some things that God demands of you and me insofar as we are Christians; God may or may not demand these of people who are not Christians. Third, there are demands usually associated with the idea of vocation that are typically phrased as "God wants me to be a physician" or "God has called me to teach." (We need to sort out whether we think God calls us to *be* something, to *do* something, or both.) Finally, some demands are those unique to you and to me, to our situations in the world, and to the moment, like God's call to Vickie Perkins to give her shoes to the barefoot woman.

How do I know what God wants me to do? Adding the partners' responses together, our process of discernment would include reading and hearing the Scripture, being told directly by God or Jesus, paying attention to where we are in the moment, and examining our gifts and our roles in our communities. It would also include noticing the various feelings and desires we have, pondering whether we would have thought of an experienced demand on our own, having discussions with people we trust, praying, and making exploration a habit (at one point, I called this "education"). Some of these practices are more foundational than others, which we discuss later.

The process of moving from this point to your statement of a final conviction is not necessarily an easy one. Sometimes the pieces fall together quickly, but often you will find yourself struggling to decide how to balance the various partners and how to weigh their many answers. It may also be difficult to see how to include earlier hypotheses and convictions that have been important to you and how to conclude this process with a conviction that speaks to your heart. There are no firm principles or guidelines to use in balancing all of these things. The tools for theological assessment that we have seen along the way can help you to explore the possibilities, but the final choice on these issues of balancing and juggling is yours. Rest assured, though, that the more you practice the theological process, the easier and more natural it becomes.

As I put all of the pieces together, here is the final conviction that emerges for me: *God demands action from us. There are at least three kinds of demands: general demands to all Christians, more specific demands to individuals to fulfill certain roles for which they are gifted, and unique demands in the moment. These are God's ways of loving us and loving the world. With training, we can learn to hear God's demands, to trust and respond to them, and to love on God's behalf.* Given that I have shared with you most of the material and all of the processes that lie behind this conviction, you may find that you accept it yourself, or you may see important places where you must, with clear and sufficient reasons, disagree. As I briefly explain this conviction and offer some good reasons for accepting it, consider whether your final conviction differs from mine, and, if so, how you would justify your alternative version. Write your view so you can remember and work with it.

❧⟐❧⟐❧⟐❧⟐❧⟐❧

Notes

❧⟐❧⟐❧⟐❧⟐❧⟐❧

The idea that God demands action from us flows, with some qualifications, from everything that we have said. The notion of three kinds of demands is a combination of my own early gut reaction to this problem of vocation as well as our conversations with the partners. The real essence of my conviction is the third sentence and comes, in part, from my own understanding of the highest ethical claims we can make on behalf of God and the world. In my view, there is nothing higher or more important than love to God's way with us and our way with one another. The final sentence also flows from everything we have said, though I have made it more specific. It reminds us that, in our own experiences and in those of our Christian sisters and brothers, we can mishear or fail to act on what we hear clearly. It also reminds us that these missteps are not the only possibility for us— that we have the possibility to do better.

Above, I noted briefly that "demand" seems to me a better characterization of what we experience of God than "invitation." "Demand" carries the weight of "you must respond." I think back on the stories we heard, and the determined quality of God's call strikes me: Perkins's use of "God appoints," Carol's experience of the "hound of heaven," Vickie's sense of the consequences of not listening well, Jesus' appearance to Paul, God's conversation with Moses—all of these echo God's persistence and insistence that what is demanded be done. God is not just inviting us to do something and leaving the rest in our hands; God is demanding that we live our lives in a certain broad way or that we act in a certain particular way. The freedom to do what God demands or do otherwise is not removed from us, but it is clear that only one of these would be the correct choice.

Many of us are uncomfortable when we are faced with demands. We do not like being told what to do. However, one implication of this conviction is that there may well be right and wrong ways for each of us to live, both broadly speaking and in very specific circumstances. In addition, the demands God makes are one of God's ways of loving us. When we live in the ways that God demands that we live, we find, even if not immediately, that we are bettering both the world and ourselves. These demands are gifts to us that enable us to be fulfilled as the individual human beings and Christians we are; at the same time, they help God to re-create the world. Vickie speaks of receiving blessings when she hears and follows God correctly. Perkins sees the common good as the point of vocations, an external result that mirrors our own personal happiness at living the life we are intended to live. According to our conviction, this is simply the way that God works. In the end, then, to use a biblical metaphor, as we give our life, we save it.

Love is an overused and sometimes misleading term. It can be used to express strong liking, as in "I love peanut butter" or "I love my Manolo Blahniks." It can also be used as an excuse for horrible exercises of lust and power. Used appropriately, however, "love" captures the very highest in human morality and ethics. As the active seeking of what is best for the other, it is unsurpassed in moral thinking and action. To love God and love neighbor is often seen as the heart of Christian living; compassion and the ideal of the Bodhisattva are reasonably considered parallels in Buddhism. Love does not, here, preclude justice or other high moral ideals, but surrounds all of them with the grace that gives them purpose and point. When we follow God's demands, we cooperate with God's loving of the world and of us. God loves you by gifting you with your purpose when you discover your vocation; God loves the world because your true purpose contributes to the true well-being of others. If you believe some other idea is a higher or more complete moral concept, you should use that in your conviction to describe what God is doing. For me, though, there is nothing greater than love.

One of my favorite authors made this point with respect to vocation decades ago. Thomas Merton, in *No Man Is an Island*, wrote, "All vocations are intended by God to manifest His love in the world."[2] All that God demands of us is for this reason, whether it be our vocations or some immediate demand. That point is not new, but new or old, neither the fact that I have made the point nor the fact that others before me have made identical or similar ones means it is a point, a conviction, on which you can or must base your life. It does, however, fall to you to decide whether to base your life on this conviction.

God's demands come to us in at least three forms, and there may be others. According to the tradition and the experience of Christians, God demands many things of Christian people, including and perhaps most importantly that they love God and neighbor. This is the chief general demand God places upon us. Although this demand sets the tone for our discussion of the other two forms, by itself it tells us little. For each one of us is different, each one of us is uniquely gifted, and each one of us must love God and neighbor in the specific way we are called. In this light, God calls some to teach, some to parent, some to heal—in whatever ways God can love the world. Finally, God's demands come to us episodically and individually; for example, I am called to help the homeless man on the street before me and you are called to send more money than you thought you had to the Red Cross for disaster relief. Always, God's love is exercised in the moment; sometimes, demands come in and apply to a moment alone.

You know that a significant part of the Christian tradition has put the second of these types of demands in the category of vocation. We see this well represented in Perkins and in much contemporary Christian conversation. I see these callings more as actions or sets of actions than as roles. I prefer, for example, to speak of God's demand that *someone teach* rather than that *someone be a teacher*. This is not a mere matter of semantics. It is rather a reflection of my concern that we (1) should separate vocations and ways of making a living, a common separation in talk about vocations, and that we (2) should not get ourselves in the bind of having to wonder, for instance, whether God has created just the right number of teachers to live in New York City at just the right time in history. To say we are called to teach, or to heal, or to minister, or to build, or to design, or to parent, or to serve our country is not to associate us necessarily with any one career path or societal role.

As we have discussed, God can be misheard. Further, acting on the demands we perceive, even when we are pretty sure we perceive them clearly, is often not easy. Moses protested, the rich young man went away grieving, Perkins says to stay put until you are sure, Vickie admits she cannot always follow, Carol shares her struggles with shifting her whole life around; the process is often not an easy one when we try to figure out what, exactly, is being demanded of us and try to muster the courage to act on it. Discerning on one's own is an inherently risky business, and acting on one's own takes more strength than most of us have. This is why it is important that Christians become part of discerning communities. Before discussing this, however, we need to confirm that our conviction does what faith convictions are supposed to do.

Six Conditions of Well-Formed Convictions

Having undergone rigorous theological assessment, all final faith convictions will meet several conditions. These have not been in one place before, but you have seen all of them. Be sure, as you review them now, that you can affirm their importance.

The first three conditions emerge from the very nature of faith itself. In chapter 2, we saw that to live by faith is to rely upon a set of articulable but frequently unarticulated and unconscious convictions that provide us with the personal resources necessary for living well in an uncertain world. From the accompanying discussion there, we can conclude that well-formed faith convictions:

1. Help us to make sense of, and give meaning and purpose to, the world and ourselves.
2. Help us to live well in the midst of our uncertainties.
3. Create a better world when we live them rather than other important alternative convictions.

The next condition includes the requirements that the conviction fits within the broad parameters of the Christian tradition, responds to some of the issues to which Christian conversations respond, and is shaped by what the conversation partners have learned. Thus, well-formed faith convictions:

4. Can be seen as meaningful and integrated parts of the Christian conversations to date.

The final two conditions emerge from the discussion of critical and ethical guidelines in chapter 3. We have been applying both of them, especially the first one, in our discussions along the way. Here we state them explicitly. Well-formed faith convictions:

5. Can withstand critical examination.
6. Are consistent with and, perhaps, expressive of, the highest moral value(s) we can imagine.

To withstand critical examination does not mean that the conviction is logically invincible, if such a thing is even possible when one is speaking theologically. Instead, it means that any doubts we have about the conviction on critical grounds are not so severe as to make it unacceptable as a ground on which to base our lives. The doubts I might have about the personlike quality or the omnipotence of God, for instance, do not make it impossible for me to affirm that I believe in God; they simply require me to do some interpretive and reconstructive work when I say who God is to me.

What do you take to be the highest moral value(s) we human beings can imagine? You have seen my answer: love. Whatever God is doing in the world, presumably God would not be God unless God were acting in the highest moral ways possible. We may well not know those ways, so our best bet is to put our faith in the highest moral values we can. This is as close to knowing God's way of being or acting as we are likely to get. My continuing sense is that understanding love as the active seeking of what is best for the other is the principle that deserves our adherence.

In the last several pages, you have seen me make a number of claims about God that I appeared deeply reluctant to make earlier. I am portraying God as an episodic interventionist who relates to us personally in a number of ways to prompt us to love the world on God's behalf. That does not sound much like the skeptical (even if passionate) author of earlier chapters. The more skeptical side reemerges, however, as we remind ourselves of the nature of theology.

As far as we can know, faith stops short of the reality of God. We cannot be certain that our faith convictions touch the divine. Theological analysis is not the study of God; God, assuming there is one, may or may not be accessible to us. God-talk is, as far as we can know, about us, about human beings. We *hope*, but cannot be sure, that it reaches all the way to God (whether that is an infinite distance or no distance at all), but without the possibility of certainty, theological analysis must be seen as reflection upon human convictions. Theology's aim is to provide us with the best convictions on which to base our lives. Earlier, when we substituted shorthand statements about God for the more complete statements about us that made up our hypothesis, we were jumping from something we can meaningfully evaluate to something we must simply admit is beyond our capacity to explore. This should not be a surprise to you, given the previous chapters, but it is not the way most faith discussions and theological reflections appear to proceed, so we need to remind ourselves of it from time to time.

What, then, does my final conviction mean? (*God demands action from us. There are at least three kinds of demands: general demands to all Christians, more specific demands to gift-bearing individuals to fulfill certain roles, and unique demands in the moment. These are God's ways of loving us and loving the world. With training, we can learn to hear God's demands, to trust and respond to them, and to love on God's behalf.*) If these things of God are beyond our ability to explore, how could it possibly make sense to commit ourselves to such extreme claims as this conviction includes?

Think of it this way. If we take an event or experience or other apparently basic feature of human living, and if putting it in God-language helps us to make sense of, and give meaning and purpose to, ourselves and the world, if it helps us to live well in the midst of our uncertainties, can be seen as a meaningful part of Christian conversations to date, withstands critical examination, is consistent with or even expressive of the highest moral values we can imagine, and if it creates a better world in the living of it than important alternative convictions, we can and should describe it as God's work. We can and should put it in the God-language of our ongoing Christian tradition. We can and should commit ourselves to its truth, for it is the best we human beings can ever do at reaching the reality of God. If our highest reaching in rationality, morality, and imagination is not the closest to God that we can get, then we are truly lost, for we have no idea what or who or whether God might be.

A feature of our place in the world that cannot be ignored is that we are always responding to what is given. Yes, we do make choices and shape the world, but never by starting from nothing. We are always responding to the environment, to felt needs and interests, to aches and pains and elatedness, to other people and what they do, and to a sense that what is given is bigger than we are. Sometimes we experience a nagging, an urging, a pulling or prodding, a calling. At other times, we feel a demand quality from interests that seem to be growing within us and that we cannot and do not want to deny. They get stronger and stronger and become a different kind of demand. Other demands come from the societies or communities in which we live. Whatever the experiences may be like, we must respond to them somehow: whether we try to ignore them or fight them off or run from them or heed them, we must answer the call . . . if a call it is.

One of the ways we who are Christians have found to make sense of these experiences is to put them in the larger context of God's work in the world. This may or may not mean that God is the efficient cause of any given one of them—remember, we are not looking for causal explanations here—but they are somehow part of the way the world is structured within God's larger purposes. The experiences and, thus, our lives, are given meaning and purpose beyond ourselves when we see these demands as part of God's work.

What is God's work? What is God doing in the world? The Christian tradition offers a story that has to do with reconciling the world to Godself after the fall (each of us needs to assess that in some other time and place), but it has often seemed to me as though the simple point is that God is loving the world, loving you and me, seeking the very best for us. I have sometimes referred to myself as a "love fundamentalist" because I see love as the highest ideal that can be sought. This is why, I take it, God is sometimes seen as Love and God's work in Christ is seen as loving the world: the highest we can conceive we attribute time and time again to God. Given this, what else could God be doing but loving the world? And what else could

God's demands be about? The answer is "many things," because to say that love is fundamental is not to say that it is the only thing going on; yet if our callings are to give purpose to our lives, this is the highest possible purpose and the one we should take them to fulfill. This is why we not only must train in discernment, but we must train in love. Anything we think we discern that is not loving in the sense of seeking the good for the other is something of which we should be extremely suspicious.

Can our conviction that the demands we experience are the demands of God withstand critical examination? Yes and no, and this is where the deepest uncertainty of our lives comes into play. Yes, for all the reasons we have seen in these paragraphs; no, because of the doubts I expressed about such notions as God intervening episodically in our lives. In the end, we cannot commit ourselves to a highest conceivable truth—that than which nothing greater can be conceived, in the words of St. Anselm—if the God of our conception produces something that we cannot rationally accept. For me, the most pressing question, and one I think I want to answer affirmatively, is whether a God who is *not* personlike can demand or call.

We could, of course, remove the God-language from our conviction and even the idea of God from our context and hear, in this way, conversation partners who deny the reality of God. This is where we each must bet our lives on something that we cannot demonstrate is or is not better for the world to believe. Indeed, by betting our lives in one direction or the other, we obligate ourselves to make the world better from that perspective. Much good and much evil have been done in God's name, and those who think we should dispose of the idea of God altogether are not unreasonable people. Indeed, they are betting their lives on one direction. I bet mine, for obviously autobiographical and other reasons, on the ultimate truth of something like the reality of God and God's love for the world, but I could be wrong. My responsibility, then, is to be sure that the world *is* a better place in the God context than outside of it; if that cannot be done, I will, from a human perspective, be proven wrong. How well can I love the world and how well can I do it in God's name? That is the Christian question and the way we should measure our past, present, and future. If not better in this way than the other important alternatives, then perhaps Christianity has failed. Our final question, then, is one that must be lived out: does our proposed conviction create a better world in the living of it? If it does not, then, as difficult as it may be, we need to discard it. Our conviction's real quality and consequences can only be known as we live it.

To begin to understand what living this conviction would mean, we focus in the next section on discernment. What would our lives look like if we were to take such discernment seriously? If my conviction is true as stated, how do you discern what it is God wants you, in particular, to do?

Discernment

When one friend was trying to discern her next step in life, she made a list of all the careers in which she had ever had any interest. Over the course of a year or two, she narrowed the list by crossing off possibilities. From time to time, of course, she also added new possibilities to the list. When she finally decided on attending graduate school in theology, she had crossed off such things as private detective, interior designer, architect, plumber, matchmaker, and math teacher. Depending on your point of view, hers was either a very thorough or a very chaotic discernment process. In the end, she found her direction and, several months later, is happy with her decision. Through it all, her central question was, "What does God want me to do?"

For Christians, this is a common question. It arises when we are sixteen, eighteen, twenty, or forty and are trying to decide on our first or second career. It arises when we are twenty-five or seventy-five and want to know whether this man or this woman is the one we should marry. It arises when we attempt to discern what percentage of our income or assets we should give to our church or to charity. It may arise when we decide what classes to take, whether to attend college, which college to attend, how many children to have, whether to go to work or to call in sick so we can help a friend in need, which mission trip to take, where to go on vacation, which spiritual practices should be part of our lives, how we can best help a family member in need, whether to have sex before marriage, whether or not to be a vegetarian, which car to buy, how to deal with a child's problems at school, how to confront a friend who is living irresponsibly, or whether to speak up during a meeting. The more our faith convictions are integrated into our lives, the more likely we will be to ask this discernment question when we face small daily decisions as well as huge life-changing ones. Sometimes when we ask the question, we have experienced one or another demand and are attempting to understand its meaning. At other times, we only know that we have a decision to make, and we are looking for guidance. Whatever the situation, our goal is to be sure we are doing what God wants, not what God does not want.

The most important thing to notice at this point is that our conviction will shape our answers. This is a crucial point. What you believe about God and what God is doing will have a profound effect on what you hope to see and what you do see when you ask, "What does God want me to do?" Through all of the work in this book, we have come to a place where we (or at least I) can say that God works in such a way that we can experience various demands for us to act in certain ways as being God's love for the world—or, in other words, that this understanding of God serves us and the world well. Our process of discernment, which includes learning how to recognize the signs of these demands and the nature of love, depends upon our faith conviction. Should we be wrong about that, our way of discerning and what it is we think we are discovering could well be wrong. If we see the demand-quality of life as a psychological matter and not a theological one, our approach to discernment will change. If we believe that God is not concerned with loving the world, then we are likely to act differently than if we believe love for the world is central to God's being. This is why working hard to articulate and defend appropriate faith convictions makes such a difference; we base our lives on these things. This point should make clear the necessity of doing solid theological work if we are to discover God's ways, or the closest we are likely to come to them.

Thus, theological reflection is foundational to discernment. But whose theological reflection counts? To be frank, you are only going to listen for God according to your own claimed theological vision. You may, and should, listen to others, including your conversation partners, but you will ultimately live according to what you as an individual Christian person believe. That is why so much of this book is directed to each of us as individuals as we try to think theologically and to live faithfully. Our transition to the topic of discernment, however, reminds us of the importance of community for the Christian life. Faithful Christian communities are the context within which theology and discernment must be done, for they train us in the lifelong practices that make discernment and faithful living possible.

Richard Foster, well-known author of such works as *Celebration of Discipline*, writes about praying for the healing of others. He cautions about the importance of beginning one's practice by focusing on illnesses that are not serious.[3] His point, at least in part, is that the spiritual life is a progressive one. This is as true about discernment as it is about healing prayer. Although God will do what God will do (or insights will happen as they happen), we cannot plan on being able to discern how we should live our lives without learning from those who know, which means being immersed in an appropriate kind of Christian community.

Implicitly, of course, we all practice discernment communally. The theological views of any one of us are the result of thousands of years of theological work and the input of countless clusters of people. Christian theology and Christian practices do not emerge into our awareness from nowhere. Instead, the interactions of millions of people over the centuries come together in each one of us in some unique way or other but with common themes and implications. What shapes us implicitly can be made explicit. We should accept the influences that continue to shape us by claiming the power of community in our lives and finding communities of faith in which to practice our theological exploration and our discernment. Committing to be an active part of a community that takes seriously the practice of listening for and living out God's demands will enable you to practice Christian life more comprehensively than perhaps any other single commitment you can make.

I am not saying that you have to go to church. While spending some years in church is surely the best way to incorporate into your life the ideas and practices that create the context for the kind of theological reflection we have been doing, many churches are not especially good at promoting either serious theological reflection or serious group discernment. Sadly, many people have not had good experiences with congregations in their lives; others have searched through many congregations, house churches, Bible study groups, and parachurch groups and have not found a place where they can be safely vulnerable and theologically nurtured. On the other hand, you may be part of the best congregation or other Christian community that you can imagine. Whether you are looking to create a community from friends or colleagues or are hoping your current community can support you fully in knowing what God demands of you, certain characteristics make possible the kind of discernment required by our conviction. In addition to a commitment to deep and sustained theological reflection, which we have already mentioned, and in addition to a basic understanding of and commitment to the Christian story, which has been assumed throughout the book, we can add truthfulness, vulnerability and acceptance, openness to God (the ability and willingness to recognize the demand-quality of reality and to act accordingly), and love of the creation. This may or may not be a complete list, but the conditions are necessary ones.

Truthfulness

The point of lying is to create worlds alternate to the one in which we actually live. If I lie to you, I am trying to convince you that the world is somehow a different place than it is. Whether or not a lie is told with good intentions, it will be very difficult to justify when told to a group of Christians who are seeking to live in accordance with the demands God is placing on us. Distorting what we see and hear through lies told to our community may not only violate the community's spoken or unspoken grounding principles; it may also violate God's purposes for someone's life. If I lie about the gifts I see in you, I run the risk of putting you on the wrong track in your life, which undercuts the entire purpose,of the discerning community. Truth telling sometimes requires uncomfortable confrontation, but this is why a real discerning community can be so difficult to build. In this light, it is worth remembering Stanley Hauerwas's caution that the virtue of peacemaking incumbent upon Christians sometimes requires that our communities be confrontational: ". . . peacemaking is that quality of life and practices engendered by a community that knows it lives as a forgiven people. Such a community cannot afford to 'overlook' one another's sins because they have learned that such sins are a threat to being a community of peace."[4]

Acceptance and Vulnerability

We cannot assist one another in the important task of discerning God's demands on our lives without being vulnerable to one another. This does not mean that our community acts as a therapy group, but it does mean that we need to share relevant facts of our lives with one another when doing so benefits the discernment process. We will have a difficult time recommending a correct course for you when you ask whether you should propose to your significant other if you do not share with us that you are still in love with someone else. If you continue to insist that God is demanding that you repeat the same action over and over many times each day, without telling us that you are struggling with obsessive-compulsive disorder, we will not be able to give you helpful input. And you will need to talk about the deep joy you experienced on your mission trip to Jamaica in order for the community to help you to sort out your career options.

At the same time, each community must make being vulnerable safe. We cannot ignore the possibility that God will sometimes call any one of us to repentance through the kind of process Hauerwas discusses, but the recognition of such a call should occur within the community's overall context of loving-kindness to one another. A group of church educators I worked with a few years ago was a bit shocked when I suggested that a person should be able to stand up in church and ask for the community's discernment around the issue of whether he or she should be sexually intimate with a boyfriend or girl-friend. Both at the level of vulnerability and at the level of accep-tance, this suggestion seemed insane, but it cannot be. If we are honestly and deeply committed to discerning how God would have us live, then no dimension of human life can be off-limits for chal-lenging and loving discussion with our discerning communities.

Openness to God

As I noted above, openness to God means being able and willing to recognize the demand-quality of reality and to act accordingly. When I talk about the community being open to God, then, I mean that it sees some faith conviction about being open to God as being well formed. When we seek a community that is open to God or seek to make our community open to God, then we are looking for a com-munity that understands that God works in the world, at least in part, through giving us certain demands. And we seek a community that makes a priority out of hearing these demands and supporting one another in the process of accepting and acting on them.

A Christian community of discernment will be able to teach new members how to pay attention to God's calling, as well as how to dis-cover when God is calling and when God is not. Since such teaching is accomplished primarily through *doing* and not through *telling*, in part because of the potential uniqueness of God's address to unique individuals, I cannot produce a sure set of guidelines. However, we can look back to our conversation partners and see how they identified certain experiences and reflections as indicators of God's demands. The list includes deep joy and contentment, a feeling of rightness, analysis of our gifts, and synchronicities. All of these, along with deep distress or discontentment, feelings of wrongness, and trusted others telling us we do not have certain gifts, should be watched for as we try to be open to God. We should remember here that the end we seek is never the stubborn insistence on our own way, but the clear affirmation that one way of living our life is the way that God has lovingly chosen for us.

Love of Creation

At the heart of what God demands is love. One of the things we seek in our discerning community is practice in the art of discerning and doing what is most loving. A good community practices these things internally, in loving one another, and externally, in loving the world. It is accustomed (or devoted to becoming accustomed) to hearing God's demands that the world be loved in certain ways. It understands that our individual gifts are sometimes the way God points us to unique ways we are called to love ourselves and others. As you form the habit of loving others in your life and in the moment, being open at the same time to receiving God's love through others, you become more able to discover the way of loving that is most characteristically yours—that fits with your gifts and deepest joys.[5]

While these words sound good, they may disguise the profound difficulty we have in practicing love. Sometimes loving is hard because it is difficult to see what is best for the other person. Sometimes it is because we feel empty ourselves and do not have the strength to love someone else. Sometimes it is because doing what is truly best for another would make that person angry. Sometimes it is because we cannot see through our own ego-needs sufficiently to really love the other. Sometimes it is because we cannot figure out a way to balance two calls to love before us. Sometimes it is because we cannot make sense of the notion that we are to love such a large and abstract thing as a nation or the environment. And sometimes we just wonder when it is finally going to be our turn to be loved; we are tired of giving all the time. Without making the solution to these dilemmas seem too easy, they are part of the point for Christian community. Without others to love us, without others to support and encourage us, we do not have the strength, courage, or wisdom to love well. Individuals should be cautious about trying to follow God's apparent demands to love without the communal network that all human beings need to sustain that love over time.

Frequently Asked Questions

The uniqueness of each of our individual situations and the individual ways God calls to us make it nearly impossible to illustrate a process of discernment that would be transferable to any given situation. Below, I am going to try to address some questions that are frequently asked when people speak with me about vocation. My answers are brief, but I hope they at least suggest to you directions for continued exploration of your own life and God's demands for you.

Is there always just one answer to the question of what God wants me to do?

Not always. It is reasonable to assume that there are some situations in which there is one and only one right thing to do. Some situations are that narrowly defined. However, if you find that you are called to teach, for example, it may well be that there are many ways of life in which you can fulfill this call. Will God call you to a specific expression of your teaching gift? There is no way to know this in advance, but not necessarily. I believe that I am called to teach theology at Hanover College, but each layer of that belief is less certain than the one before it. I am less convinced that I am called to teach at Hanover than I am that I am called to teach theology. I am less convinced that I am called to teach theology than I am that I am called to teach. Even my conviction that I am called to teach is not beyond question. God may leave many routes open to us.

If I feel completely at home doing a particular thing, is that my vocation?

Feeling completely at home is one of the signs for which you might look as you seek to understand what kind of life God demands of you. At the same time, our access to God is not sufficiently guaranteed that we can make any one discernment tool determinative of how we live. We can mistake being lazy and insufficiently challenged for feeling at home. We can feel at home for our own personal reasons of convenience rather than for God's reasons. You should pay close attention to your experience, but you should also use all of your other important tools in conjunction with your discerning community.

Does God have a vocation in mind for everyone?

Put in that way, of course, the only possible answer is that we cannot know. If, on the other hand, we ask whether the conviction that would correspond to this question is a well-formed one, then it leads to some very important reflections. Given the conditions under which so many live in our world, if God does have a vocation in mind for everyone, we would have to explore whether some of us are responsible for helping to create conditions under which the very poor, for instance, can discern and live their vocation. We would also have to explore to what extent God's demands are relative to our situation: does the rich person have a different set of demands to hear than the poor person, based on these economic differences? There are not too many issues more important than these involving social justice.

What am I going to do next?

This is one of the most common discernment questions we ask. To answer it, the most effective approach we can take is to pose it to that community of fellow seekers who know us well and who have been trained in practices of discernment. Even within that context, however, it must be narrowed down. Ask yourself: What do I already know about my gifts and desires? Where do I find joy? How has God worked in my life in the past, and what does this suggest about how God might be working now? Where do I see demands in my life? What are some potential ways I can imagine myself contributing to God's loving the world? These questions are the kinds you should be asking. Be patient. Go slow. Do not be afraid to take a small step and see what happens. Trust that the answer will emerge in time.

Does it matter what I do, as long as I treat people well?

Not everyone is convinced that there is such a thing as a particular call. Rather, they say, you can do whatever you want to do; you just have to love people wherever you are and whatever you are doing.

God demands that we love our neighbor, but not that we do this within a particular context. Again, this is a claim that hinges upon our acceptance of a certain faith conviction about God and what God is doing in the world. My, and maybe your, conviction includes the possibility that you and I are called to some particular way of life as God's way of loving the world. I urge you to continue to explore and test that conviction and that implication in your own living.

Is every demand that I experience a call from God?

No. At least there is no reason to suppose so. I feel something like a demand, tug, or pull to get up and head into my office even when I do not have any morning appointments scheduled and could easily write at home. I do not see God in that demand, and my faith conviction does not rest upon doing so. I can experience a desire to have coffee in the morning that feels like other demands I would call God's demands; I have much more reason to assume this is about my caffeine addiction than about anything God is doing in the world. Various emotional and physical and even spiritual needs can create the experience of demand, but without there being an intelligible connection to God. The quickest test in these kinds of cases is whether we can honestly and plausibly connect our experience of demand with the love we know lies at the root of God's relationship with us and God's calls to us. Again, of course, trusted and experienced friends often hold the solution to our puzzle in these difficult cases.

Parting Words

I do not expect these brief answers to resolve the issues raised, but I hope they make possible your own pursuit of more complete answers. If you work through each theological issue you raise using the process illustrated in the book, and if you work with a community of discerners toward seeing how you are best suited to cooperate in God's loving of the world, you cannot go far wrong.

In the end, we do not commit ourselves to convictions; we commit ourselves to God. The problem is that we cannot know whether it is really God to whom we are committing ourselves, because we are committing ourselves by way of a certain set of experiences and concepts that may or may not accurately reflect whatever or whoever God is. So we construct the very best and highest convictions we can and commit ourselves to acting in accordance with them as we continue to explore them and our other convictions throughout our lives. This is the way of the Christian. It is the only way possible for us. It is an excellent way, for it means we always strive to be on the side of love and always strive to be open to hearing the God who, in the end, we remain convinced loves us. I wish you clarity of mind and heart and the support of a discerning and nurturing community as you journey into your future with God.

Questions for Reflection

1. Could God be a cat? Why or why not? (If that question seems absurd, think of it this way: how do we rule in and rule out certain ways of thinking about God? What makes an image of God a good or appropriate image?)
2. I have specified several conditions that any well-formed conviction must meet. Do you agree with my conditions? Would you add or subtract any?
3. How would you pull together the various comments from our partners? Do my four questions capture accurately what they are trying to say?
4. Do you see any evidence that God is loving or not loving the world? Is this a trick question in theology?
5. What is love?
6. Are you part of a discerning community in the sense I have described it? Why or why not? Will you be part of such a community in the future?
7. After reading this book, how do you think I would answer the question, "Why should one be a Christian?" Do you find my answer to be persuasive? Why do *you* think one should be a Christian?
8. Are you experiencing any lasting demands these days? Does God seem to be trying to get through to you somehow? How will you discern what God wants to say to you? How will you gather the courage to respond according to God's demand?
9. Christians live and die by their faith. You are engaged in the process of developing your own Christian theological stance. How is this process related to life and death?
10. What does God want you to do with your life?

Notes

Chapter 1: A Skeptical, Passionate Faith

1. Gordon D. Kaufman, *In Face of Mystery: A Constructive Theology* (Cambridge: Harvard University Press, 1995). I might also have seen this first in "Theology: Critical, Constructive, and Contextualized," which is chapter 2 in Kaufman's *God, Mystery, Diversity: Christian Theology in a Pluralistic World* (Minneapolis: Fortress Press, 1996). I first read both of these about a decade ago. I went back to *God, Mystery, Diversity* after I completed this book, and I noted the extent to which Kaufman's views influenced me. I am grateful to him for his work.

Chapter 2: Defining Faith and Theology

1. Jonathan Kozol, *Amazing Grace: The Lives of Children and the Conscience of a Nation* (New York: HarperPerennial, 1995).
2. John Calvin, *Institutes of the Christian Religion* 3.2.7; ed. by John T. McNeill, trans. Ford Lewis Battles, LCC (Philadelphia: Westminster Press, 1960), 1:551.
3. William P. Alston, *Perceiving God: The Epistemology of Religious Experience* (Ithaca, NY: Cornell University Press, 1991), 277.
4. The Apostles' Creed. For the complete version, see, for example, the Presbyterian *Book of Common Worship* (Louisville, KY: Westminster John Knox Press, 1993), 65. The Nicene Creed is on p. 64.
5. The complete *Ave Maria*, central to the saying of the Rosary, is, "Hail Mary, full of grace, the Lord is with thee. Blessed art thou among women and blessed is the fruit of thy womb, Jesus. Holy Mary, Mother of God, pray for us sinners, now and at the hour of our death."

Chapter 3: Partners in Christian Conversations

1. Allen Verhey, *The Great Reversal: Ethics and the New Testament* (Grand Rapids: William B. Eerdmans Publishing Company, 1984). See especially 169–74.
2. I am indebted to Philip Barlow for most of this paragraph, as I am for so many other theological and personal insights.
3. For a classic treatment of the Atonement, see Gustaf Aulén, *Christus Victor: An Historical Study of the Three Main Types of the Idea of the Atonement*, trans. A. G. Hebert, foreword by Jaroslav Pelikan (New York: Macmillan Publishing Co., Inc., 1969).

4. For additional information on war as well as many other issues, see James F. Childress and John Macquarrie, eds., *The Westminster Dictionary of Christian Ethics* (Philadelphia: Westminster Press, 1986).

5. My thanks to my dear friend Amy Schultz for allowing me to use these passages from two e-mails that she sent to me, one on June 1, 2004, and one on June 7, 2004. She has given me more love, grace, and insight through the years than I can even begin to mention.

6. See Diana L. Eck's *Encountering God: A Spiritual Journey from Bozeman to Banaras* (Boston: Beacon Press, 1993) for a more complete discussion of these approaches to other faith traditions, especially the chapter, "Is Our God Listening?"

7. For some discussion of the Bodhisattva, see any good introduction to Buddhism. Consider Kogen Mizuno's *Basic Buddhist Concepts*, trans. Charles S. Terry and Richard L. Gage (Tokyo: Kosei Publishing Co., 1987), as a brief possibility.

Chapter 5: Vocation, Part 1

1. I have written about my indebtedness to all those associated with the PTEV projects elsewhere in this book. Here, I simply want to note that I use the expression "theological exploration" many times in this book. I take it it is not a trademarked phrase, but I certainly absorbed it from my work with Lilly Endowment, so it seems only fair to give them the credit for putting the words together in a way that caught and kept my attention.

2. This prayer can be found on p. 50 in the Presbyterian *Book of Common Worship* (Louisville, KY: Westminster John Knox Press, 1993).

3. One accessible book on Christian meditation is Ken Kaisch, *Finding God: A Handbook of Christian Meditation* (New York: Paulist Press, 1994).

4. See John Shelby Spong's interesting discussion of people praying for the healing of his wife in *Why Christianity Must Change or Die: A Bishop Speaks to Believers in Exile* (San Francisco: HarperSanFrancisco, 1998), 141–42.

Chapter 6: Vocation, Part 2

1. Stanley Hauerwas, *Unleashing the Scripture: Freeing the Bible from Captivity to America* (Nashville: Abingdon, 1993). The quotations in this paragraph are from p. 15. My thanks to Dave Cassel for his friendship and for numerous helpful comments on this chapter.

2. Wiliam C. Placher, ed., *Callings: Twenty Centuries of Christian Wisdom on Vocation* (Grand Rapids: William B. Eerdmans Publishing Company, 2005).

3. William Perkins, *A Treatise of the Vocations, or, Callings of men, with the sorts and kinds of them, and the right use thereof,* in *The Workes of That famous and Worthy Minister of Christ in the Universitie of Cambridge, Mr. William Perkins. The First Volume: Newly corrected according to his own Copies* (London: 1616). This *Treatise* was originally published in 1602. I have not thoroughly compared this 1616 printing with the 1602 version or

the 1605 version that the reader can find on Early English Books Online; there are only spelling differences in the particular passages quoted. The 1616 printing that I used may be found in the archives at Wabash College, and I thank Beth Swift, archivist, for her assistance. Further references are by page number in the text. I have made no attempt to make Perkins's language inclusive, preferring that we read what he wrote.

4. This interview was conducted on August 9, 2005. My thanks to Vickie for allowing me to use it and for her ministry to me over the years. I have made no attempt to inclusivize her language.

5. Many thanks to Carol for allowing me to use this wonderful story, which she first sent to me by e-mail on July 20, 2005. I have not made the language inclusive.

6. Eugene H. Peterson, *The Message: The Bible in Contemporary Language* (Colorado Springs, CO: Navpress Publishing Group, 2002).

7. Michael Novak, *Business As a Calling: Work and the Examined Life* (New York: Free Press, 1996), 39.

8. This quotation is from a paper Jay wrote for an upper-level ethics course entitled Christian Calling that he took with me in the winter of 2005. I greatly appreciate his willingness to allow me to use it here.

9. Diana L. Eck, A New Religious America: How a "Christian Country" Has Become the World's Most Religiously Diverse Nation (San Francisco: HarperSanFrancisco, 2001).

Chapter 7: God, Love, and Vocation

1. My thinking about vocation has always been focused around such issues and questions. See, for instance, my "Constructing a Theology of Vocation," in *Inquiries* 2, no. 1 (Fall 2001). *Inquiries* is a publication of Hanover College's Center for Free Inquiry. I am grateful to the Center for inviting me to present an initial version of this paper at their March 2001 symposium, "Job, Career, or Vocation: Defining Work for the Twenty-first Century."

2. Thomas Merton, *No Man Is an Island* (San Diego: Harvest, 1983), 153.

3. See Richard J. Foster, *Prayer: Finding the Heart's True Home* (San Francisco: HarperSanFrancisco, 1992), 206

4. Stanley M. Hauerwas, "Peacemaking: The Virtue of the Church," in *Christian Existence Today: Essays on Church, World and Living in Between* (Durham, NC: Labyrinth Press, 1988), 91.

5. One of the most frequently cited characterizations of vocation is from Frederick Buechner: "The place God calls you to is the place where your deep gladness and the world's deep hunger meet." See *Wishful Thinking: A Seeker's ABC* (San Francisco: HarperSanFrancisco, 1993), 119. We certainly want to be careful about how we define gladness and hunger, but the sentiment is a powerful one.

Suggested Reading

I have put together these lists to encourage you to continue your theological explorations. I tried to choose books that satisfy two criteria: (1) they are accessible to you, should you wish to read them on your own or with a small study group, and (2) they will enable you to explore more deeply and in different ways some of the issues you began to explore in this book. You will discover, as you read, that these authors do not always agree with me or with one another; I hope you find the variety of perspectives stimulating.

A brief look at these topical lists reveals two additional things. First, I have listed books under one category that could fit within other categories as well. This should deepen your reflections on the relationships between various theological topics and on possible ways to balance the various conversation partners. Second, virtually all of the books I have listed here have been published in the last forty years. To expand the list beyond that time frame would quickly make it unmanageable, but you will find many earlier sources referred to in these books.

I hope you will enjoy asking questions of these books and letting them ask you questions. I hope you will try out various answers to your theological questions and see which ones make your life most meaningful and enable you to contribute most lovingly to the world. I also hope you have fun reading. This material is important and sometimes life-changing, but it can also be very enjoyable.

Entries with an asterisk are those I consider to be more difficult to read than the others.

Bible

You want, of course, to be reading the Bible itself along with material that helps you to think about what it is and what it means. The New Revised Standard Version, New International Version, and New Jerusalem Bible would be good translations with which to begin.

Peter J. Gomes. *The Good Book: Reading the Bible with Mind and Heart*. New York: William Morrow and Company, Inc., 1996.
Thomas Merton. *Opening the Bible*. Collegeville, MN: Liturgical Press, 2000.
Chaim Potok. *In the Beginning*. New York: Alfred A. Knopf, 1975.

Discernment

Frederick Buechner. *Sacred Journey: A Memoir of Early Days*. San Francisco: HarperSanFrancisco, 1982.

Tilden Edwards, *Living in the Presence: Disciplines for the Spiritual Heart*. San Francisco: Harper & Row, Publishers, 1987.

Suzanne G. Farnham, et al. *Listening Hearts: Discerning Call in Community*. Rev. ed. Harrisburg, PA: Morehouse Publishing, 2000.

Richard J. Foster. *Celebration of Discipline: The Path to Spiritual Growth*. 10th ann. ed. Rev. and exp. San Francisco: Harper & Row, Publishers, 1988.

Tony Hendra. *Father Joe: The Man Who Saved My Soul*. New York: Random House, 2004.

John S. Mogabgab, ed. *Communion, Community, Commonweal: Readings for Spiritual Leadership*. Nashville: Upper Room Books, 1995.

Ethics

°Tom L. Beauchamp and James F. Childress. *Principles of Biomedical Ethics*. 4th ed. Oxford: Oxford University Press, 1994. The first two chapters are an excellent review of ethical terms and theories.

Carol Gilligan: *In a Different Voice: Psychological Theory and Women's Development*. Cambridge: Harvard University Press, 1982.

°Stanley Hauerwas. *A Community of Character: Toward a Constructive Christian Social Ethic*. Notre Dame, IN: University of Notre Dame Press, 1983.

Margaret E. Mohrmann, *Medicine as Ministry: Reflections on Suffering, Ethics, and Hope*. Cleveland: Pilgrim Press, 1995.

Faith

The books by Coffin and Lamott are nonfiction, while the others in this section are novels. I often find that fiction moves me most when pondering what it means to live with and by faith.

William Sloane Coffin. *Letters to a Young Doubter*. Louisville, KY: Westminster John Knox Press, 2005.

Susan Howatch. *Glittering Images*. New York: Fawcett Crest, 1988. This is one of many Howatch novels you might enjoy.

Laurie R. King. *A Monstrous Regiment of Women*. New York: Bantam Books, 1997.

Anne Lamott: *Traveling Mercies: Some Thoughts on Faith*. New York: Pantheon Books, 1999.

Chaim Potok. *The Chosen*. New York: Fawcett Crest, 1982.

———. *The Promise*. New York: Fawcett Crest, 1990.

———. *My Name Is Asher Lev*. New York: Fawcett Columbine, 1996.

———. *The Gift of Asher Lev*. New York: Fawcett Columbine, 1997.

Erich Segal. *Acts of Faith. New York: Bantam, 1993.*

God

Marcus J. Borg. *The God We Never Knew: Beyond Dogmatic Religion to a More Authentic Contemporary Faith*. San Francisco: HarperSanFrancisco, 1997.

Marcus Borg and Ross Mackenzie, eds. *God at 2000*. Harrisburg, PA: Morehouse Publishing, 2000. With articles by Karen Armstrong, Marcus Borg, Joan

Chittister, Diana Eck, Lawrence Kushner, Seyyed Hossein Nasr, and Desmond Tutu.

°Martin Buber. *I and Thou*. Translated by Walter Kaufmann. New York: Charles Scribner's Sons, 1970. This is actually a translation of a book that was published almost five decades earlier, but *I and Thou* is not to be missed.

Diana L. Eck. *Encountering God: A Spiritual Journey from Bozeman to Banaras*. Boston: Beacon Press, 1993.

°Elizabeth A. Johnson. *She Who Is: The Mystery of God in Feminist Theological Discourse*. New York: Crossroad, 1994.

Thomas R. Kelly. *A Testament of Devotion*. San Francisco: HarperSanFrancisco, 1992.

Thomas Merton. *New Seeds of Contemplation*. New York: New Directions, 1972.

History of Christian Thought

William C. Placher. *A History of Christian Theology: An Introduction*. Louisville, KY: Westminster John Knox Press, 1983.

Robert Louis Wilken. *The Spirit of Early Christian Thought: Seeking the Face of God*. New Haven, CT: Yale University Press, 2003.

Love

Jonathan Edwards. *Charity and Its Fruits: Christian Love as Manifested in the Heart and Life*. Edinburgh: The Banner of Truth Trust, 2000.

Joseph F. Fletcher. *Situation Ethics: The New Morality*. Philadelphia, PA: The Westminster Press, 1966.

Thomas Merton. *Contemplative Prayer*. With an introduction by Thich Nhat Hanh. New York: Image Books, 1996.

Henri J. M. Nouwen. *The Inner Voice of Love: A Journey through Anguish to Freedom*. New York: Image Books, 1998.

Henri J. M. Nouwen, Donald P. McNeill, and Douglas A. Morrison. *Compassion: A Reflection on the Christian Life*. New York: Image Books, 1983.

Other Faith Traditions

My first suggestion under this heading would be reading some of the sacred texts from other faith traditions. For instance, you should read the Koran, the Bhagavad Gita, the Tao Te Ching, the Dhammapada, and parts of the Talmud.

Diana L. Eck. *A New Religious America: How a "Christian Country" Has Become the World's Most Religiously Diverse Nation*. San Francisco: HarperSanFrancisco, 2001.

Rita M. Gross and Terry C. Muck, eds. *Buddhists Talk about Jesus; Christians Talk about the Buddha*. New York: Continuum, 2005.

Harold S. Kushner. *To Life: A Celebration of Jewish Being and Thinking*. New York: Warner Books, 1993.

His Holiness the Dalai Lama. *The Good Heart: A Buddhist Perspective on the Teachings of Jesus*. Translated from the Tibetan and annotated by Geshe Thupten Jinpa. Boston: Wisdom Publications, 1998.

Sogyal Rinpoche. *Tibetan Book of Living and Dying*. Edited by Patrick Gaffney and Andrew Harvey. San Francisco: HarperSanFrancisco, 1992.

Huston Smith. *The Illustrated World's Religions: A Guide to Our Wisdom Traditions*. San Francisco: HarperSanFrancisco, 1994.

M. Thomas Thangaraj. *Relating to People of Other Religions: What Every Christian Needs to Know*. Nashville: Abingdon Press, 1997.

Theology

°Anne E. Carr. *Transforming Grace: Christian Tradition and Women's Experience*. San Francisco: HarperSanFrancisco, 1988.

Catechism of the Catholic Church. New York: Image Books, 1995.

James H. Cone. *A Black Theology of Liberation*. 20th ann. ed. Maryknoll, NY: Orbis Books, 1990.

Andrew M. Greeley. *The Great Mysteries: Experiencing Catholic Faith from the Inside Out*. Lanham, MD: Sheed & Ward, 2003.

°Stanley J. Grenz and John R. Franke. *Beyond Foundationalism: Shaping Theology in a Postmodern Context*. Louisville, KY: Westminster John Knox Press, 2001.

°Gordon D. Kaufman. *In Face of Mystery: A Constructive Theology*. Cambridge: Harvard University Press, 1993. See especially the first five chapters.

Alister E. McGrath. *Theology: The Basics*. Malden, MA: Blackwell Publishing Ltd., 2004.

Daniel L. Migliore. *Faith Seeking Understanding: An Introduction to Christian Theology*. Grand Rapids: William B. Eerdmans Publishing Company, 1991.

James B. Nelson. *Thirst: God and the Alcoholic Experience*. Louisville, KY: Westminster John Knox Press, 2004.

John Shelby Spong. *A New Christianity for a New World: Why Traditional Faith Is Dying and How a New Faith Is Being Born*. San Francisco: HarperSanFrancisco, 2001.

Vocation

Karen Armstrong. *Through the Narrow Gate: A Memoir of Spiritual Discovery*. New York: St. Martin's Press, 1981.

———. *The Spiral Staircase: My Climb out of Darkness*. New York: Alfred A. Knopf, 2004.

Gary D. Badcock. *The Way of Life*. Eugene, OR: Wipf and Stock Publishers, 2002.

Wendell Berry. *Jayber Crow*. Washington, DC: Counterpoint Press, 2001.

Matthew Fox. *Reinvention of Work: A New Vision of Livelihood for Our Time*. San Francisco: HarperSanFrancisco, 1995.

Dominic Grassi. *Still Called by Name: Why I Love Being a Priest*. Chicago: Loyola Press, 2003.

Laurie R. King. *Folly*. New York: Bantam, 2001.

Thomas Merton. *Seven Storey Mountain*. New York: Harcourt Brace & Company, 1976.

Parker J. Palmer. *Let Your Life Speak: Listening for the Voice of Vocation*. San Francisco: Jossey-Bass Inc., Publishers, 2000.

William C. Placher. *Callings: Twenty Centuries of Christian Wisdom on Vocation*. Grand Rapids: William B. Eerdmans Publishing Co., 2005.

Wayne Teasdale. *A Monk in the World: Cultivating a Spiritual Life*. Foreword by Ken Wilbur. Novato, CA: New World Library, 2002.